WHAT THE
Industrial Revolution
DID FOR US

WHAT THE
Industrial Revolution
DID FOR US

GAVIN WEIGHTMAN

BOOKS

This book is published to accompany the television series
What the Industrial Revolution Did for Us, first broadcast on
BBC2 in 2003.

Series producer: Patricia Wheatley
Executive producer: Jonathan Stamp
Production coordinators: Patricia Bowker and Caroline Schafer
Series directors: Simon Baker, Jonathan Hassid and Billie Pink
Series researchers: Sarah Jobling, Nancy Strang and Edwin Blanchard

Published by BBC Books, BBC Worldwide Ltd,
Woodlands, 80 Wood Lane, London W12 0TT

First published 2003
Text copyright © Gavin Weightman 2003
Introduction copyright © Dan Cruickshank 2003
The moral right of the author has been asserted.

ISBN 0 563 48794 1

Commissioning editor: Sally Potter
Project editor: Patricia Burgess
Art director: Linda Blakemore
Designer: Janet James
Picture researcher: Caroline Wood
Indexer: Patricia Hymans
Production controller: Belinda Rapley

Set in Garamond by BBC Worldwide Limited
Printed and bound in Great Britain by Butler & Tanner Limited, Frome
Colour separations by Radstock Reproductions Limited, Midsomer Norton
Jacket printed by Lawrence Allen Limited, Weston-super-Mare

For more information about this and other BBC books,
please visit our website on www.bbcshop.com

330·942

Contents

Introduction

The epoch of the Industrial Revolution was Britain's heroic age. Men and women of astonishing ingenuity, inventive power and sweeping vision appeared on the scene. Within a few fleeting decades, from 1760 to 1840, the old modes of life and work – in many ways little advanced since the Middle Ages – had given way to the modern world we know today.

The advance took place on many fronts, and in many different fields the same names appear. It was the age of the polymath, of the new Renaissance man, with many different fields of endeavour linked by the common thread of the open, inventive and enquiring mind. In Britain, technology and art were fused, and in their creative combination contrived to astonish the world. Culture and commerce were in an easy and fruitful alliance. There was no inherent contradiction in the mind of great and pioneering manufacturers, such as Matthew Boulton, between the creation of personal wealth and an almost visionary determination to benefit mankind through the application of new technology. It was a time when new machines, such as Richard Arkwright and Jedediah Strutt's cotton-spinning water-frame, not only produced traditional materials at greater and more economic speed, but also in improved quality. The result, ideally, was that higher-quality merchandise was produced more rapidly and cheaply, making what had been expensive luxuries, such as porcelain crockery or fine cotton fabric, available to a far wider range of the population.

There is no doubt that life in the new mills – organised around revolutionary but noisy and demanding machines – was tough and highly disciplined. For example, at Arkwright's epoch-making Cromford Mill in Derbyshire, children worked thirteen-hour shifts with machines operating day and night for six days a week. But these mills, mass-producing wares that were in great demand at both home and abroad, also guaranteed employment. When the quest for profits ruled supreme, and in a world where workers' rights were hardly protected by legislation, exploitation by employers could be extreme and conditions appalling, especially in the intrinsically dangerous and physically demanding mining industry. But when production was overseen by such enlightened entrepreneurs as Arkwright, the workforce was offered not just regular wages but security, dignity and a fate far better than the alternative that had faced much of Arkwright's workforce – life within the sterile and humiliating confines of the parish workhouse.

During the decades of the Industrial Revolution, the world in which people lived came under new scrutiny. This was the age of discovery, of objective

Opposite: A forge in Blackburn, Lancashire, painted by James Sharples, an engineer and self-taught artist towards the end of the eighteenth century. One of the most important innovations in the Industrial Revolution was the smelting and forging of iron with coke rather than charcoal, which freed the industry from reliance on woodland and allowed for a huge increase in production.

observation, of the questioning, investigation and exploration of nature and the natural world. The greater understanding of the human body, of diseases and treatments that came of this knowledge led not only to advances in medicine, but also to a better and more profitable understanding of the planet. Suddenly, after millennia, the secrets of the Earth were revealed, and the key to great wealth came within the grasp of man. New perceptions about the nature of geology made it possible to identify the location of valuable mineral resources, while new technology – particularly improved steam engines – made it possible to dig deeper than ever before to win the treasures of nature, such as coal, clay or copper, from the bowels of the Earth.

The cast list in this great adventure is fascinating and revealing, as is the dazzling array of amazing machines, products and ideas that rapidly emerged and changed the world for ever. The explosion of activity that took place after 1760, and that was only characterised as the Industrial Revolution over one hundred years later, had its roots in the very early years of the century. In a sense, the modern world of industrial manufacture, of mass-production and engine-driven machinery, started in a picturesque river valley in Shropshire. In 1709 in Coalbrookdale – a location rich in the raw materials of the nascent industrial age, including coal and iron ore – Abraham Darby solved the problem of producing high-quality iron suitable for casting a wide range of industrial, military and domestic products. Coke, produced from coal, was the key, and three years later Thomas Newcomen utilised the new technology and discoveries of the age to produce the first powerful and effective steam engine. Suddenly it was possible to gain practical access to rich mineral resources, especially coal, buried deep underground. Newcomen's coal-fired steam engine was used to pump subterranean water from mine workings that could now go deeper than ever and win coal from places that had previously been inaccessible. The mass-production of cast iron, and the first workable steam engine, marked the dawn of the age of industry, invention and discovery. Certainly, without the strong cast iron necessary for the production of machines, and without steam power – essential to work the machines and to gain access to vital natural resources buried deep underground – the Industrial Revolution would never have happened.

Coal and iron plus steam and water power formed the great heart of the revolution. The four elements united in an unprecedented manner to produce steaming and thundering 'fire engines' (as early steam engines were called) that fed on the Earth's rich coal, to forge a new world. And, if the four elements, working together in a way never dreamed of before, formed the foundation of the Industrial Revolution, then its greatest single raw material was cotton. The social and economic history of cotton is extraordinary and literally woven into the very fabric of the Industrial Revolution. From the Middle Ages Britain had, along with the rest of Europe, been a land of wool. People worked it, wore it and traded it: wool was a source of great wealth. During the seventeenth and early eighteenth centuries, silk from China or India became fashionable and a sought-after luxury, but, in the first decades of the eighteenth century, very little cotton was imported, and virtually none woven in Britain. Indeed, this great Asiatic product was viewed as a grave threat by native silk and wool weavers, and bitterly resisted; indeed, its importation and manufacture in Britain was banned for much of the first half of the eighteenth century. But the onslaught of cotton could not be stopped. Handsome, strong, increasingly cheap, and easy to wash and maintain, cotton was the material of the new, rational and modern age. It drove expensive and hard-to-wash silk and heavy wool from the marketplace so that, incredibly, by the 1830s British-made cotton – woven, of course, from imported raw material – made up 50 per cent of the fabric exported abroad. Wool, once England's commercial pride, made up only 15 per cent of Britain's exported fabrics.

The success of the cotton industry owed much to the fact that it was rapidly industrialised. In the 1730s the process of weaving was accelerated by John Kay's invention of the flying shuttle, then, in the 1760s, the process of converting cotton into thread or yarn was sped up to an incredible degree by James Hargreaves' spinning-jenny, and then by Arkwright and Strutt's water-frame, one of the great wonders of its age. It not only produced vast amounts of thread at high speed – spun and wound in one process – but, for the first time in Britain, made thread strong enough to allow the production of full cotton fabric.

The machines invented and developed for the cotton industry not only helped to make Britain the richest nation in the world by the 1830s, but also created the form of Britain's industrial architecture and, to a large extent, its industrial towns. Early mills or factories, such as those at Cromford in the 1770s, were organised around the requirements of the power source and the machines they housed. These buildings were ruthlessly practical and utilitarian in a way virtually unknown before the eighteenth century, and of huge scale. This was truly the age of the engineer, driven by the practical demands of the machine and not by aesthetics alone. The mills were, essentially, machines designed to house machines and, as such, were pioneering examples of pure, functional architecture, utterly fit for their purpose. Ironically, the sublime scale of these mills perfectly captured the artistic mood of the period, obsessed with romantic notions of the picturesque and the 'awful'. The mills – rising

9

tall, ablaze day and night – created a powerful and poetic image of the modern world.

The stories in other fields of manufacture, invention and endeavour are equally enthralling and impressive. In the world of manufacturing and mass-production, the charismatic Matthew Boulton – at his massive and elegant Soho works in Birmingham – turned out high-quality and affordable consumer goods for the emerging middle classes, including buttons, buckles and other fashionable 'toys'. He presided over a profound social change. The increasing wealth of the nation meant that large numbers of people had money to spend not on necessities, but on fashionable luxuries. This was the birth of consumer capitalism. Boulton even, in the 1790s, started to produce the nation's copper coinage – to a far higher and forgery-proof standard than could be achieved by the Royal Mint. He also, through his manufactory, got deeply involved in power supply, and, during the 1780s, was instrumental in persuading the taciturn James Watt to improve the efficiency of the steam engine and, crucially, to adapt it to power a wide range of new machines.

Josiah Wedgwood was one of the manufacturing wonders of the age, who, by the late eighteenth century, was selling his high-quality, exquisite and mass-produced pottery throughout the world. Wedgwood, as he manufactured his antique-style Etruscan ware, embraced not only art, archaeology, commerce and technology, but also the worlds of geology and discovery. The quest had long been on in Europe to discover the secret of fine and highly prized Chinese porcelain. Was it the material used or the method of manufacture – or both? The man who found the Chinese formula for true porcelain could make a fortune. In 1750 came the breakthrough, achieved in true Industrial Revolution style. William Cookworthy, an apothecary with a bright and enquiring mind, realised that the secret of porcelain lay in the type of clay used – kaolin – and came across a native supply while inspecting a Newcomen engine in Cornwall. Britain's high-quality china industry was born, and boomed to such a degree that imports of Chinese porcelain – the value of which had peeked at £73,000 in 1763 – had declined to almost nothing by 1800.

As manufacturing boomed, inland communications became all important. Transport had to be improved, rapidly and radically, if the trade potential of the Industrial Revolution were to be fully realised. First roads, which, if anything, were worse in 1750 than they had been in Roman times, were upgraded, and some fantastical characters rose to the demand of the moment, including the almost mythic 'Blind Jack' Metcalf. Despite his blindness, Metcalf was a man of extraordinary vision when it came to roads – he could 'feel' the land to determine the best route, calculate everything in his head, and, during the 1760s and 1770s, gave Yorkshire the best roads in Britain. No less extraordinary was John McAdam, who, in 1816, at the age of sixty, became Britain's greatest road builder, and whose name became synonymous internationally with smooth, strong, firm and well-drained roads.

At the same time the nation's canal system was created, pioneered by daring engineers of intuitive knowledge, such as John Brindley. In the 1760s the visionary Brindley conceived Britain's first arterial canal, which cut through or bridged over the existing landscape rather than merely following its natural contours. This bold approach to engineered transport anticipated the railway age in which lines would be cut in a similarly uncompromising manner through the landscape. And the railway age was not long arriving, and very much the child of the decades of the Industrial Revolution, even if its greatest exploits were achieved in the following Victorian Age. Richard Trevithick created the first steam-driven vehicle, and at Christmas 1801 drove it around the roads of his native Camborne in Cornwall. Trevithick adapted the machine for rail, creating the first railway engine in 1804, but then he and his futuristic project rather ran out of steam, and it was not until 1825 that George and Robert Stephenson's trundling and puffing *Locomotion* initiated Britain's first railway, running the 9 miles between Stockton and Darlington. And then, most pioneering of all, in 1784 the epoch saw the birth of the age of flight, with Vincent Lunardi's epic two-hour journey in a hydrogen balloon from central London to Hertfordshire. This was followed in 1804 by the flight of a glider, designed by George Cayley, that in its aerodynamic form and configuration established the principles of the modern aeroplane.

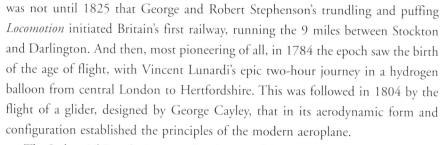

The Industrial Revolution was also the age of the last great feat of exploration: the quest for the mythical Southern Continent, traditionally called *Terra Australis Incognita*. Industrialisation and exploration were intimately connected for Britain, bursting, as it was, with manufactured goods and energy. It needed new colonies that would provide markets for manufacturers to exploit, and havens where raw and profitable materials and commodities, such as cotton or tea, could be found or grown in plantations. Dutifully, Captain James Cook, along with botanist Joseph Banks, set sail on the *Endeavour* in July 1768 on a scientific journey of discovery that would, ultimately, solve the puzzle of the Southern Continent and add Australia to the British Empire.

Such long journeys of discovery into unknown waters required two very important things – a means of accurate navigation, and a food supply that would keep the crew healthy. Both these problems were solved during the Industrial

Revolution. In the 1760s John Harrison, after decades of toil, finally perfected an accurate 'longitude' clock, or chronometer, that would enable navigators to determine their east–west bearings. The clock came too late for Cook to take one with him on the *Endeavour* in 1768, but he had one with him in 1772 when he set out on his second epic journey, and later described it as his 'faithful guide'.

The solution of the health problems on long sea journeys forms part of the extraordinary story of medicine in the industrial age. For medical men, the late eighteenth century was a period of speculation and experimentation in which haphazard inquiry only gradually gave way to scientific method, analysis, organised research and clinical trials. The treatment for scurvy, the scourge of long sea journeys, is a prime example of the new rational approach to medical treatment. Scurvy was a killer, yet the cause of the disease was a complete mystery to medical men, and various, often wild and outlandish, treatments were suggested. Then, in 1754, a Scottish naval surgeon called James Lind subjected the six most favoured treatments to a controlled, rational and clinical test. This was the spirit of the dawning age of the Industrial Revolution in action. Of the twelve scurvy seamen tested, those treated with oranges and lemons recovered rapidly, while the rest did not. Lind, and this was typical of medical knowledge at the time, had no way of discovering why the treatment worked (vitamin C was not identified for over 200 years), and – also typical of the age – Lind's treatment was not fully recognised and applied for another forty years.

But medical progress had been made, with myth and superstition being replaced by objective, scientific testing. A similar new and scientific approach to disease led to the taming of the greatest killer of the age – smallpox. Edward Jenner, aware that immunity to the disease was possible, observed that milkmaids never caught smallpox, and made a brilliant lateral leap. They were exposed to cowpox, so could this disease be related to smallpox and provide immunity in a safe manner? His observation led, in May 1796, to the first vaccination being administered. It worked, and with this success, a new age of medicine arrived. By 1799, over 5000 people were vaccinated in England alone.

Similar speculation, observation and experiment led to other significant scientific and medical discoveries. For example, in the 1790s Joseph Priestley, a nonconformist preacher with an enquiring and radical mind, set himself the task of investigating the effect of heat on different substances. By heating mercuric oxide he isolated and, for the first time, identified something he called 'dephlogisticated air'. Through further experiments he realised that he had discovered the 'stuff of life', but then the somewhat bemused amateur discoverer moved on to other things. It was left for another scientist, a few years later, to name Priestley's discovery 'oxygen'. An archetypal product of the Industrial Revolution, who joined with like-minded thinkers in the Lunar Society, Priestley saw connections in all things, particularly between radical politics and science. He was a great supporter of the French Revolution because he believed its notions of freedom and equality were a reflection of natural laws: all men were, he observed, equal under the laws of medicine and science.

The age of the Industrial Revolution was also the age of war, with Britain struggling to subdue its American colonists during the 1770s and 1780s, and then taking on Revolutionary and Napoleonic France from 1793 to 1815. War concentrates the mind, and the inventive spirit of the age came up with a host of improved and pioneering inventions and materials. These included the submarine, the rifle, the first detailed map of Britain (the Ordnance Survey intended to give British troops the edge over the invading French), and easy and cheap-to-make wrought iron and cement. And technology developed for military purposes was rapidly transferred to other uses; for example, ironmaster John Wilkinson's method of accurately boring cannon was later used to create cylinders for steam engines.

If there is one emblem of the Industrial Revolution, it is the city. Workers were pulled from the country into towns and, with the arrival in the late eighteenth century of efficient and diverse steam power, mills and factories could abandon their reliance on water power and move from remote and rural valleys into more convenient urban locations. The great early nineteenth-century product of this shift was Manchester, with its clusters of huge and high-rise cotton mills. But London was the focus, and, by the first decade of the nineteenth century, it had become the largest and greatest city in the world: the new Rome – the new Babylon. And it was primarily the creation not of princes or of aristocrats, but of speculators, informed builders, men of commerce and financial imagination – men, indeed, of the Industrial Revolution. Whole quarters in east London, along the Thames, were laid out as walled towns of warehouses, created to store the wealth of the world brought home to Britain. New building technology – cast-iron columns, windows and doors, and stone and brick walls and floors – were used to achieve security, vast storage capacity and fire protection in these sublime warehouses that, like all the best products of the Industrial Revolution, combined utility and function with refined beauty. And the creators of these warehouses were engineers rather than architects: George Gwilt from 1799 at the West India Docks, D. A. Alexander from 1800 at the London Docks, Thomas Telford and Philip Hardwick during the 1820s at St Katharine's Dock.

The robust, simple and elegant beauty expressed by these great warehouse complexes, combined with a machine-like visual repetition and the aesthetic of mass-production, characterised the great developments that transformed London during the era of the Industrial Revolution. The Bedford Estate and Foundling Estate in Bloomsbury, built from the 1770s to the 1830s, were impressive products of the age that saw speculators, builders, architects, landlords and legislators working together to produce the new city for the industrial age. John Nash's creation from about 1812–30 of the picturesque Regent's Park terraces and villas, Regent's Street, Oxford Circus and Piccadilly Circus was the urban wonder of the age – a fairy-tale land of palaces set in park, and splendid uniform, neo-classical terraces clad with stucco and painted to look like expensive stone. The development created genteel housing, fashionable shops, markets and neat workers' housing where previously there had been fields and slums. These innovations in urban design and construction were refined and developed by the builder Thomas Cubitt, who, during the first half of the nineteenth century, built up vast swathes of London, catering for a broad spectrum of society, and introduced the idea of the all-embracing building contractor, who controlled design, construction, infrastructure and the supply and testing of materials.

And so the modern city, starting to be brightly lit by coal gas and served by water delivered under pressure in new cast-iron water pipes, had arrived. It was all part of the modern world – the world we inhabit now – that was the creation of those great and gifted inventors, manufacturers and engineers of the Industrial Revolution. This book reveals what they did for us.

Dan Cruickshank
July 2003

Author's Note

Among the new and fascinating features on the tourist map of Britain in the second half of the eighteenth century were its mines and mills, canals and ironworks. The foreign visitor, on tour as much for instruction as idle pleasure, would include in an itinerary of the Lakeland Hills and Arundel Castle a visit to some of the wonders of the 'machine age'. A French geologist, Faujas St Fond, for example, was thrilled by the clamour of industry in the north-east of England:

> This beautiful river the Tyne, is rendered highly interesting by the number and variety of manufactures carried on on its banks. On one hand are seen brickfields, potteries, glass-houses and chymical works…on the other manufactories in iron, tin and every kind of metal… This…diffuses everywhere so much activity and life…that the eye is agreeably astonished in contemplating such a magnificent picture. Humanity rejoices to see so many useful men finding ease and happiness in a labour which contributes, at the same time, to the comfort and enjoyment of others…

St Fond was touring Britain in 1799, which was about the halfway point in what would later be known as the Industrial Revolution, and which undoubtedly laid the foundations for the 'comfort and enjoyment' of millions – though hardly with easy and happy labour. Had St Fond toured Britain thirty years earlier, he would have found very little in the way of manufacture that differed from his native France. And had he returned just thirty years later, he might have travelled on a steam railway, or even a steam wagon puffing along, not on iron rails, but on one of John McAdam's newly laid roads.

Much of what appears to us now as comical or downright polluting, was a source of wonder in the period from about 1760 to 1840. Travellers from all over the world flocked to the deep and wooded gorge of the river Severn in Shropshire to see the ironworks of Coalbrookdale and the world's first cast-iron bridge put up in 1776. Although the roaring fires and smoke of the furnaces were described as hellish, it was the sheer energy of the place, forging boilers for steam engines that ran mills and pumps and hammers, that impressed the visitor.

Nobody at the time thought of all this as a 'revolution'. As one innovation spawned another in the making of cloth or the creation of new kinds of crockery, and as mills appeared above the rural landscape, and mines were dug deeper, a new world emerged without anyone being able to comprehend what it all amounted to. It was only when it had happened that, looking back, historians tried to make sense of the forces that had been unleashed and called it the Industrial Revolution. The term first became popular in England in 1884, when the young historian Arnold Toynbee wrote a series of Lectures on the Industrial Revolution.

The term had been familiar in French and German writing much earlier, and it seems likely that Toynbee, with an interest in social reform, came across it in the works of Karl Marx. There, and in the writing of Marx's collaborator and patron Friedrich Engels, it meant more than rapid social and economic change. The French Revolution of 1789 had promised to overturn political life, and offered new freedoms: the Industrial Revolution would, in time, transform the whole of society when the workers got hold of the 'means of production'. Toynbee did not use the term 'industrial revolution' in that way: he was just trying to make sense of what had happened to Britain between the end of the eighteenth century and the beginning of the nineteenth.

We tend today to think of the Industrial Revolution as essentially Victorian, and it was certainly in the mid-nineteenth century that it reached its zenith. But it began much earlier, and was more or less complete in all its essentials by the time of Queen Victoria's coronation in 1837. All the great innovators and entrepreneurs – from Richard Arkwright and his cotton mills to James Watt and Matthew Boulton with their steam engines – travelled in horse-drawn coaches on turnpike roads, regarded new canals as the very pinnacle of modernity and engineering skill, and witnessed a consumer revolution in which the wearing of cheap cotton clothing and the drinking of tea from English 'china' was novel enough to be remarked upon.

It is still hard to take in the magnitude of the changes that occurred. In 1761 the Society for the Encouragement of the Arts, Manufactures and Commerce staged the first-ever exhibition of ingenious machinery in Britain. On display were model ships, showing the latest methods of rigging, and every other contrivance driven by wind, water or 'gin' horses, which spent their working lives harnessed together and walking in endless circles. Only one exhibit, known as a 'fire engine', was powered by steam. A good deal of the industrial plant on show, such as spinning-wheels, was still worked by hand. The society had put up a prize for a new kind of spinning machine that could produce more than one thread at a time, but there were no takers.

Just ninety years later, when the same Society for the Encouragement of the Arts, Manufactures and Commerce promoted what became known as the Great

Exhibition in the Crystal Palace at Hyde Park, the 6 million people who visited between May and October 1851 wondered at the steam-driven world on display. Many arrived in London by steam train, and some American tourists had crossed the Atlantic in paddle-steamers. Whereas coal had hardly featured in 1761, at the entrance to the Crystal Palace was a 24-ton lump of it symbolising the new source of British power.

What the Industrial Revolution Did for Us is a journey back in time that charts the ways in which British life was transformed in the seventy years or so before Queen Victoria came to the throne. Although there was terrible hardship in the mills and the mines, the end result was the creation of a world in which the luxuries of the rich were offered in real, but modest, terms to the many. Despite the gloomy prediction of the Rev. Thomas Malthus in his *Essay on Population* (1798) that the rapidly rising population of industrial England would lead to 'vice and misery' unless there were some 'restraint', the multitude was housed and fed. An estimated population for England and Wales of 6–7 million around 1750 had risen to 9 million at the time of the first population census in 1801, and to 18 million by 1851. This was made possible by a huge increase in the supply of food, and by a domestic revolution that came about with the mass-production of everyday necessities.

The most evocative piece of machinery produced by the Industrial Revolution was undoubtedly George and Robert Stephenson's huffing and puffing *Locomotion*, which, in September 1825, pulled six loaded coal cars and twenty-one cars carrying 450 passengers on the 9-mile railway between Stockton and Darlington to the cheers of a crowd 40,000 strong. That is more or less where this history ends. But the more humble kettle, singing on the hearth and ready for a brew of tea to be drunk from a china cup, could just as well stand for what the Industrial Revolution did for us. This book, and the BBC television series it accompanies, takes us back in time to marvel alongside eighteenth-century observers at the newness and invention of it all.

Gavin Weightman
July 2003

17

CHAPTER ONE

A Potent Brew

The radical journalist William Cobbett, born the son of a tavern-keeper in Farnham, Surrey, in 1763, regarded the fashion for tea-drinking, which had swept through Britain during his lifetime, as an abomination. In his book *Cottage Economy* (1822) he spluttered with rage at the wastefulness of the whole procedure, compared with the humble tankard of home-brewed ale it had replaced in national affection.

It is notorious that tea has no useful strength in it; that it contains nothing nutritious… It is, in fact, a weaker kind of laudanum, which enlivens for the moment and deadens afterwards. It is, then, of no use. And now, as to its cost, compared with that of beer, I shall make my comparison applicable to a year, or 365 days. I shall suppose the tea to be only five shillings the pound, the sugar only sevenpence, the milk only twopence a quart. The prices are at the very lowest. I shall suppose a teapot to cost a shilling, six cups and saucers to cost two shillings and sixpence, and six pewter spoons to cost eighteen pence. How to estimate the firing I hardly know, but certainly there must be in the course of the year two hundred fires made that would not be made, were it not for tea drinking. Then comes the great article of all, the time employed in this tea-making affair. It is impossible to make a fire, boil water, make the tea, drink it, wash up the things, sweep up the fireplace and put all to rights again in a less space of time, upon an average, than two hours.

By the early Victorian period, tea-drinking had replaced home-brewed beer as the national tipple. The radical journalist William Cobbett complained that the time spent preparing and drinking tea was wasteful and sapped the 'national energy'.

18

In condemning the drinking of tea, Cobbett very nicely defines the emergence of a new way of life that had first begun to take shape towards the end of the eighteenth century. Tea was at the very heart of it, for this was a beverage that, since the seventeenth century, had been a luxury of the well-to-do, who could afford the high price of imports from China, brought in the heavily armed ships of the East India Company. The same ships often had cargoes of fine porcelain crockery, the manufacture of which was for centuries a closely guarded secret of the inscrutable Chinese ceramicists. Now, in the early nineteenth century, the brew-up was regarded as an essential part of the day in nearly every home, mill, mine and factory.

Only the wealthy could afford to drink tea from genuine Chinese porcelain cups in the mid-eighteenth century. As industrialism took off, lower prices and cheaper English 'china' allowed nearly everyone to enjoy a nice 'cuppa'.

19

A NEW CONSUMERISM

What was once available only to the rich, was now the luxury of all but the poorest, who had their mill-spun cotton tablecloths and tea towels, and cheap crockery. In the paraphernalia of the tea table could be found in microcosm the results of more than half a century of ingenuity in transforming foreign luxuries into home manufactures that were produced in sufficient quantity, and therefore cheaply enough, for even the agricultural labourer. Charles Dickens has many a character find solace in the Chinese leaf, and recognised its universal appeal. In *Pickwick Papers* (1837) Sam Weller and his father go to a meeting of the Brick Lane Branch of the United Grand Junction Ebenezer Temperance Association:

> On this occasion the women drank tea to a most alarming extent; greatly to the horror of Mr Weller senior, who, utterly regardless of all Sam's admonitory nudgings, stared about him in every direction with the most undisguised astonishment. 'Sammy,' whispered Mr Weller, 'if some o' these here people don't want tapping tomorrow mornin', I ain't your father... Why, this here old lady next me is a drownin' herself in tea.'

The Industrial Revolution, so much associated in our minds with dragon-like, steam-driven machinery, was just as much a 'consumer revolution', which might be symbolised by the kettle singing on the hearth. British inventors and manufacturers learnt the skills that had once been the secrets of the East – India and China – and found a way of replicating them with raw materials drawn from new and cheaper sources. They invented machines that multiplied, tens or hundreds of times, the output of goods that were once homespun and handmade, and created a global market for their new manufactures. All this was achieved in an astonishingly short period: just over half a century, between the 1760s and the 1830s.

Much of the technology changed little: ships were still powered by sail and wind, and goods were hauled on land in wagons drawn by oxen and horses. But what did change dramatically was the source of power to drive machinery. This did not happen overnight: the harnessing of Britain's abundant supplies of 'sea coal', as the mined rock was generally called, was the result of the ingenuity of many practically minded inventors.

FUEL FOR INVENTION

Up to the seventeenth century, charcoal – made by slow-burning coppice wood to remove its impurities – was commonly called 'coal'. Another name, therefore, had to be given to the fuel composed of fossilised woodland compressed in layers of rock. It was known variously as 'pit coal', 'earth coal', 'stone coal', 'peacock coal' (because of its glistening appearance) and 'smithy coal' (because blacksmiths used it). But the name that gained widest currency was 'sea coal', perhaps because it was first gathered on the beaches of north-east England, where the sea broke chunks of it from exposed seams, and the tides washed them ashore. Or possibly it was because this coal was normally carried by ship. Whatever the true origin of the term, there is no doubt that the use of sea coal, as opposed to charcoal, has a very long history in Britain, and that by the seventeenth century it was not just being picked up off the beach: coal-mining had been a significant industry for quite some time.

As far back as 1366, when construction work was going on at Windsor Castle, the clerk of works put in an order for 600 tons of coal to be shipped down from a Tyneside mine at Winlaton. It was to be used to burn lime, which, along with

Filling tea chests in the 1820s. The tea trade with China was huge by this time, before the establishment of plantations in India.

sand, was an essential material for 'soldering' parts of the castle together. The coal trade then was haphazard; to get his supplies the Windsor clerk had to organise everything himself, from the keel boats ferrying the coal down the river, to the labourers who manned them, the ships carrying it down the east coast and up the Thames, and the men who unloaded it. However, over the next two centuries, the north-east coal trade, with London its largest market, became well established. Send a message to the mayor of Newcastle and he would arrange to deliver all the coal you needed: an order for 3000 tons of it to be shipped to Boulogne in France for the king's harbour works was no problem for Newcastle merchants in the mid-seventeenth century. Indeed, in 1651 the satirical poet John Cleveland wrote:

England's a perfect World! Has Indies too!
Correct your Maps: New-castle is Peru.

By the early eighteenth century, the coal trade was huge. In his *Tour Through the Whole Island of Great Britain* (1724) Daniel Defoe wrote:

I need not, except for the sake of strangers, take notice that the City of London and parts adjacent…is supplied with coals, therefore called sea coal, from Newcastle upon Tyne and from the coast of Durham and Northumberland… All these coals are bought and sold on this little spot of Room Land at Billingsgate and though sometimes, especially in the case of war and contrary winds, a fleet of five hundred to seven hundred sail of ships comes up the river at a time, yet they never want for a market… This trade is so considerable it is esteemed a nursery of our best seamen.

One such seaman was Captain James Cook, about whom there is more later (see pages 42–7).

By the eighteenth century coal was burnt in domestic fires, and the leading chefs of the day decreed it better than charcoal (they claimed it made the meat more succulent). It was also used by dyers, glass-makers, blacksmiths and workers in the woollen industry. For a while some high-grade coal was even carved into fashionable jewellery, just as jet would be the following century. It had myriad uses, was potentially far more abundant than firewood, peat or charcoal, and had only one big drawback: most grades of sea coal gave off a choking smoke. The search for a smokeless fuel went on for more than a century, and briquettes made from powdered coal mixed with earth were widely advertised.

IRON AND COAL

The one manufacturer who could not substitute coal for charcoal was the ironmaster. Although many attempts were made to smelt iron with the very best grades of coal, impurities always ruined the end-product. As a result, the iron industry, which was to be so vital for the creation of steam-driven machinery, was still confined to areas of the country that had a large supply of wood for charcoal-burning. For the most part, the wood was coppiced, that is, cut from shoots growing from a tree stump and harvested in rotation so that it was a constantly renewable resource. The industry was scattered, and evidence of this can be found in many tracts of woodland that survive to this day.

The limitations of British iron-smelting meant that much of the best-quality wrought iron was imported from Sweden, which had developed a unique system of production in its dense pine forests. British woodland was not extensive enough to compete: it had long been converted to farming because landowners could make bigger profits from sheep than from growing timber or vegetable crops. If a substitute for charcoal had not been found, a vital resource for the Industrial Revolution would have been missing. As so often in this period in British history, it was the Quakers who came up with the solution.

In the early 1700s, Britain imported nearly all its brass because the trick of combining zinc and copper in the right proportions remained a secret of the Dutch. The trade had anyway been controlled by laws that favoured London merchants and the Crown, and it was not until these were lifted that any home-grown efforts at making brass became worth while. Huge fortunes were being made in the slave trade across the Atlantic, and from trading in goods, especially brassware. Among those to profit was a group of Bristol Quakers, who decided to invest their money in what became known as the Baptist Mills Brass Works, founded in 1700. They appointed as their manager a fellow Quaker called Abraham Darby. (In those days some Quakers were involved in the slave trade, though they were in the forefront of the campaign to abolish it from the 1760s.)

Darby made a number of innovations and had attached to the brass works an experimental, and very secretive, iron foundry. He managed to cast iron in a sand mould that enabled a whole new range of lightweight pots to be produced. So that nobody could steal his discovery, Darby had the keyholes in the doors blocked. With a partner, he then took an interest in a disused iron furnace and foundry in Coalbrookdale, Shropshire. Here, in a deep gorge on the river Severn, rich in both iron ore and coal, he set up his own enterprise producing brass, copper and iron in 1709. Within a short while, Darby discovered that he could make a pig-iron smelting ore with coke. (Iron smelted with coal is made brittle by the sulphur:

23

The dramatically hellish picture of Coalbrookdale at night, as seen in 1812 by Philippe de Loutherbourg, a painter of theatrical scenery. This spot in Shropshire was, for a time, the most industrialised place on Earth.

coke is purified coal with the sulphur removed.) From this he could make such things as stoves, grates and cannon. But his coke-fired pig-iron was no good for forging into higher-quality wrought iron, which was produced by repeated hammering and re-heating. This was a serious limitation, for it was from wrought iron that various weapons, tools, screws and nails were made.

When Abraham Darby died in 1716, he had made the breakthrough, but it was another half century before his son, also called Abraham and only five years old at his father's death, developed the Coalbrookdale works further. Here he made pig-iron in coke-fired furnaces, and the end-product could be made into wrought iron. It was now cheaper to smelt iron with coke than with charcoal, and the iron

24

industry was freed from its reliance on woodland. By 1750 the Coalbrookdale works was attracting not only national, but international, attention.

One of those who visited the Darby works in the winter of 1767 was Joseph Banks, the eminent naturalist and one-time president of the Royal Society, who, the following year, would join Captain James Cook's voyage to the South Seas. In his diary Banks noted that at Coalbrookdale the furnaces 'probably cast greater quantities & better metal than any other in the kingdom…here all large casting work is done in the greatest perfection, they often cast cylinders for fire engines as large as 72 inches in diameter'. Banks was impressed by many aspects of the Coalbrookdale works, including the railway on wooden runners that delivered the manufactures into barges on the river Severn.

Coalbrookdale became a Mecca for engineers and scientists, and anyone interested in this exciting new centre of iron manufacture. The roll-call of visitors and those who contacted Darby included James Watt and Matthew Boulton (builders of steam engines), Thomas Telford and John Rennie (engineers and builders of canals and bridges), Richard Trevithick (the so-called Cornish 'giant' and steam pioneer) and Josiah Wedgwood (of pottery fame). When the furnaces were fired at night the Severn Gorge was lit up with a dramatic red glow, and many artists, including J. M. W. Turner and Philippe de Loutherbourg, who

A panorama in 1758 of the celebrated blast furnaces belonging to the Darbys of Coalbrookdale. It was here that Abraham Darby first smelted iron with purified coal or coke rather than charcoal. The 'coking' operations can be seen on the left with smoke rising, and a horse-drawn railway is transporting a cylinder for a Newcomen 'atmospheric engine'.

both worked as theatrical scene painters, captured the drama of Coalbrookdale on canvas. An Italian aristocrat, Carlo Castone della Torre di Renzionico Comasco, who visited in 1787, wrote:

> The approach to Coalbrookdale appeared to be a veritable descent to the infernal regions. A dense column of smoke rose from the earth; volumes of steam were ejected from fire engines; a blacker cloud issued from a tower in which was a forge; and smoke arose from a mountain of burning coals which burst out into turbid flames… I went the same night, following the lurid splendour of the lighted furnaces, to an adjacent fire engine, and saw the solid ironstone fused into a liquid. The machines were activated by various wheels. The noise was so great in the long tube which was joined to the furnace that it could easily be imagined the hissing of the irate furies. The stream of white hot liquid appeared as the lava of Vesuvius.

The Italian was mightily impressed with the sight of the world's first-ever cast-iron bridge forged by Abraham Darby III. He thought it a 'gate of mystery'. Completed in 1779, the iron bridge still spans the river Severn today as one of the most remarkable monuments of the early Industrial Revolution. The architectural historian Dan Cruickshank says: 'The material and pioneering means of construction are expressed in a ruthlessly honest manner quite at odds with the artistic niceties and conventions of the age. Here – in a very modern way – pure, no-frills function and utility are not only revealed but positively venerated.' The burgeoning ironworks of Coalbrookdale were in themselves impressive enough, but their greatest impact was in creating a huge increase in the demand for coal. And this in turn inspired two crucial innovations in mining.

A sketch of the wooden frame put up for the construction of the Iron Bridge at Coalbrookdale.

The world's first cast-iron bridge spanning the river Severn at Coalbrookdale. Completed in 1779, it attracted awe-struck tourists from all over Europe. This painting by William Williams shows the bridge around 1790.

MACHINES TO HELP THE MINES

A big problem for all mines, whether for copper, lead, zinc or coal, was that as the deposits near the surface were exhausted, the miners had to dig deeper. And as they dug down, surface water would begin to drain into the shafts and very quickly the mines became flooded. Water had to be pumped out with windmills, horse-powered machines or buckets on the end of ropes. In Europe, as well as Britain, inventors went to work on the problem and came up with a variety of designs for steam-powered pumps. As with all innovations, a fair bit of industrial espionage went on, but a Devonshire man called Thomas Savery, who had turned his hand to a number of inventions, devised what he called a 'fire engine' and got it patented. It was a fairly simple contraption in which steam was run into a cylinder, where it was cooled with cold water, causing a vacuum, which sucked up water from a mine and spewed it out. He built a working model, which got him a patent in 1699. This was so loosely worded as to be all-encompassing:

> A grant to Thomas Savery of the sole exercise of a new invention by him invented, for raising of water, and occasioning motion to all sorts of mill works, by the important force of fire, which will be of great use for draining mines, serving towns with water, and for the working of all sorts of mills, when they have not the benefit of water nor constant winds; to hold for 14 years; with usual clauses.

A considerable improvement on the Savery fire engine was made in the early years of the eighteenth century by another ingenious Devonshire man, Thomas Newcomen, who was a blacksmith and ironmonger in Dartmouth. Whereas Savery's engine could operate only at low pressure without exploding, and therefore worked ponderously, Newcomen's 'atmospheric engine', as it was called, overcame this problem by having an additional cylinder and piston. But Newcomen could not develop his design because of Savery's catch-all patent, and was forced to go into business with him. The first of the Newcomen steam-driven pumps was installed in a mine at Dudley Castle in Staffordshire in 1712. It was very expensive to make, calling upon the newly acquired skills of the iron-founders, but it was so effective that it was soon in great demand. It was the cylinders for Newcomen engines that Joseph Banks saw being cast when he visited

An early illustration of an 'atmospheric engine' designed by Thomas Newcomen. The first was used in 1712 to pump water from a mine. Although it could not drive machinery, it was used to top up the flow of water driving riverside mills.

The ENGINE for Raifing Water (with a power made) by Fire

Coalbrookdale in 1767, and the Darby works made more than a hundred of them. Formerly, the boilers in Newcomen engines had been made of brass, which limited their size. Now, with larger, cast-iron cylinders, they could do more work, pumping water from mines, which could be dug deeper. Although, compared with later steam engines, they were inefficient, Newcomen engines were vital in the early days of industrialism.

However, despite the claim in Savery's patent that his fire engine could drive machinery, these primitive steam-pumping machines were of limited use. Even Newcomen's improved models, which were crucial in the development of deep mines and greatly increased the supply of coal, could not be harnessed to mills that required a steady motion, and they had only a minor part to play in the rise of the industry that was to become by far and away the greatest employer of labour, and the most spectacular money-spinner, in the British Industrial Revolution: the manufacture of cotton thread and cloth.

COTTON SENSATION

Unlike coal-mining or iron-smelting, the spinning and weaving of cotton had no long history in Britain, for the nation's wealth had been founded on wool. Landowners had turned over millions of acres to the raising of sheep, which provided the raw material for most of the nation's clothing, and led to a thriving export industry in woollen cloth. Each region had its own specialism, producing varieties of woollen fabric, or mixtures of wool and linen, with names baffling to the modern ear. Daniel Defoe provided an inventory in *The Complete English Tradesman* (1726):

> The broad-cloth and druggets in Wilts, Gloucester and Worcestershire;
> serges in Devon and Somersetshire; narrow-cloths in Yorkshire and
> Staffordshire; kerseys, cottons, half-thicks, duffields, plains and coarser
> things in Lancashire and Westmorland; shalloons in the counties of
> Northampton, Berks, Oxford, Southampton and York; women's stuffs in
> Norfolk; linsey-woolseys etc at Kidderminster; dimmeties and cotton-
> wares at Manchester; flannels at Salisbury and in Wales; tammeys at
> Coventry; and the like.

Defoe makes some mention of cottons, but they were insignificant then, and pure cotton cloth was officially banned. Two Acts of Parliament had, in theory at least, outlawed the importation, weaving, making, selling or wearing of what were generally known as 'calicos'. (The name derives from the town of Calicutt on the

Malabar coast of south-west India, where the East Indiamen took on their cargoes of Indian cloth.) The government had intervened in 1721 to appease the interests of those in the wool and silk industries, who regarded imported cotton cloth as a serious threat to their livelihood, as, in time, it proved to be. If today this strikes us as bizarre, it was perfectly understandable in eighteenth-century Britain, and no different from the trade restrictions that exist today to protect domestic industries.

Until the early eighteenth century, with the exception of luxury cloth made of silk, the East wore cotton and the West wore wool or linen (made from flax). This segregation of the world had arisen chiefly from the local availability of raw materials: cotton grows only in subtropical climates, so the cloth made from it clothed the millions of India, the Middle East and a large part of Asia, but it was a rarity in Britain. However, the spice trade brought this to an end.

The East India Company discovered that the best currency for buying Indonesian spices was Indian calico. When the fortunes of the spice trade began to decline at the end of the seventeenth century, the company shipped a few consignments of patterned Indian cloth to London in the hope of opening up a new trade. Being light and compact, cotton goods were very easy to stack in the holds of sailing ships. And to the company's surprise and delight, their calicos proved an instant success. In fact, they were a sensation, and the Indian weavers and dyers were encouraged to produce patterns to fit the tastes of the London and European markets.

As more and more Indian cottons were imported, the wool and silk merchants and weavers began to protest. The East India Company was accused of threatening vital British industries. Letters, including the following one to the *British Gazetteer*, appeared in the newspapers.

> Several inhabitants of St Leonard, Shoreditch, not only weavers but divers other trades, having taken it into their consideration, and do plainly see that the wearing of callico (imported cotton cloth) will be…the ruin of the weaving trade. Now, for the discouraging of the wearing of callico, several hundreds have come to the full resolution not to buy any one thing whatsoever of any one person, after the 25th day of July 1719, that shall suffer his wife, his daughters or his maids to wear callico. And 'tis to be hop'd that all those that are lovers of our English nation will endeavour to promote our English trade.

Then the 'calico wars' broke out. In the early summer of 1719 a young woman called Elizabeth Price went looking for lodgings in Shoreditch, a district of east

London, where the clatter of hundreds of weavers' looms could be heard in the streets. As it was a warm day, many of the men had left their attic workrooms and were sitting outside, discussing the issues of the day. When they saw the young woman in her riding hood, they began to talk excitedly, for one of them saw that beneath her coat she wore a gown made of a light material, which he suspected was the very fabric that threatened his trade and that of all his fellow weavers who worked on wool and silk. Elizabeth Price, with a guinea coin for rent in the pocket of her cotton dress, was unaware that she had strayed into a hornets' nest of bitterness, and that what she wore under her cape was an incitement to riot.

Without warning, she was set upon by a mob shouting: 'Calico! Calico! Weavers! Weavers!' Her cape was torn from her and her cotton gown ripped to pieces. She was left dishevelled and distraught, her guinea lost. Price, now destitute, brought her case before the magistrates, and eventually her attackers were arrested and sent for trial at London's Old Bailey. They were charged with several acts of violence and vandalism, having also been linked to the plunder and burning of shops that sold calico, and the ransacking of a calico-printer's home.

Tried and convicted, three of the rioters were put in the public pillory at Spitalfields Market. A group of fellow weavers stood by in silent vigil, instructed by their trade association, the Company of Weavers, not to cause any more

Until the mechanisation of cotton manufacture from the 1760s, the preparation, spinning and weaving of wool and flax was a cottage industry.

31

trouble. But feelings were running so high that violence broke out once again, when a hackney carriage drew into the market and three elegant ladies stepped out, all wearing calico dresses. With their workmates suffering the humiliation of the pillory, this was too much for the weavers to tolerate. They surrounded the women and gave them the same treatment they had meted out to Elizabeth Price, trying to destroy their dresses. The newspaper *Thursday's Journal* of 6 August 1719 reported that the weavers 'offered rudeness enough to their calico and tore it pretty much, some say stript it off their backs, and sent them home to dress over again'.

In the long run, however, the violent opposition to cottons backfired. What was quite clear was that the public loved them. A clandestine industry therefore arose to satisfy that demand, and British dyers got to work to discover the secret of the fast colours used by the Indians. As cotton spun in Britain was not strong enough to provide both the warp and weft of cloth, it was often woven with linen, so the home-grown fibre still had an important part to play. Raw cotton, generally known as 'cotton wool', was of minor importance. The sure knowledge that there would be a huge demand if they could imitate, and perhaps improve on, the dazzling textiles of India was a spur to invention. But the earliest mechanisation of the industry owed nothing to new sources of power, except in so far as the rapidly growing middle-class economy was creating a demand for cheap luxury.

MACHINES FOR SPINNING AND WEAVING

The first significant innovation in the textile industry was the 'flying shuttle' patented in 1733 by John Kay, the son of a wool manufacturer in Bury, Lancashire. Weavers had previously worked the weft of a cloth through the warp strings holding the shuttle in their hand. This was not only slow, but also meant that the width of cloth was limited unless the weaver had an assistant to carry the shuttle further than he could reach. Kay's machine had a pulley mechanism that shot the shuttle back and forth. One man could therefore do the work of two, so weaving was speeded up and, as flying shuttles were widely used, the demand for thread increased.

Which of several inventors should rightly be accorded the honour of devising the 'spinning-jenny', a machine for spinning with more than one spindle at a time, is still a matter of dispute, and probably always will be. The man who got a patent for it in 1770, just as the official ban on cotton manufacture was about to be lifted, was James Hargreaves, a supposedly illiterate Lancashire weaver. He had made his first machine in 1764, but not one of the original machines survives. However, faithful reconstruction from the details of the patent application provides a good idea of what the spinning-jenny was like. For an innovation that is credited with

stimulating the growth of one of the most spectacular global industries in history, it looks totally unconvincing, more medieval than state of the art. It was crudely fashioned of wood – it is said that Hargreaves shaped most of the pieces with a penknife – and was small enough to fit inside a humble cottage. But it was incredibly effective, capable of spinning six, eight or twelve bobbins at a time, and therefore doing the work of that many spinsters working with the traditional wheel. Although it required a certain skill to operate, a child could handle it: in fact, it was thought that youngsters were more adept, just as they out-perform their parents with computers today.

Naturally enough, when the first jennies went into operation they were regarded as a threat to the livelihood of spinners, and a number were smashed. But they were very easy to make, and their value was so great that they were soon in common use. Hargreaves made the mistake of selling some jennies before he applied for his patent, so it was refused. The jennies had solved one problem – a shortage of thread for the weavers. Very soon they created another: an over-supply of thread. It was much easier to mechanise the various processes of preparing and spinning cotton from the bails of raw 'wool' than it was to find a way of powering the looms. So this was a boom time for the hand-loom weavers.

Within a few years the spinning-jenny was obsolete, as a one-time wig-maker and astute businessman Richard Arkwright devised a machine that held the tension of the threads as they spun with rollers and could be driven by a horse or water-wheel (see Chapter Two). The mechanisms of the jenny and the water-frame were then combined by Edward Crompton into a hybrid spinning system, nicknamed the 'mule', a cross between a horse and a donkey.

COTTON MANUFACTURE.

PLATE XIV

Sections of one of Mess.rs Strutt's COTTON MILLS at Belper in Derbyshire.

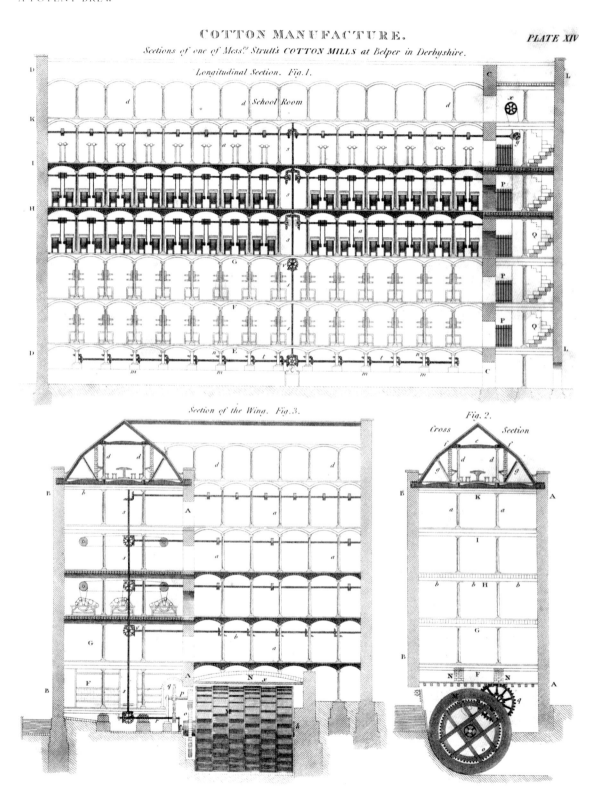

Longitudinal Section. Fig.1.

Section of the Wing. Fig.3.

Fig.2.

Cross Section

The cotton-spinners next looked for someone who could make them a steam-driven machine to power the spinning mills. Leaders in the field of economical steam pumps for the mines were by this time the partners Matthew Boulton, a manufacturer of coins and all kinds of trinkets, and James Watt, a talented but sickly and anxious Scottish instrument-maker. Newcomen's atmospheric engines used huge amounts of coal, but Watt had discovered a way of refining the steam pump to conserve fuel while simultaneously increasing the efficiency of the machine. Now, prompted by Boulton, he worked to find a way of controlling the power of the machine so that it could drive a spinning mill in which hundreds of spindles turned simultaneously. Watt had already improved on the Newcomen engine by adding a separate condenser so that the cylinder did not have to be constantly re-heated. But making an engine to drive complex machinery was another matter.

There were others who had developed steam engines that used a flywheel and could power machines. Matthew Boulton urged Watt to discover a way of harnessing their more efficient engines to the needs of industries still reliant on water power. He wrote in 1781: 'The people in London, Manchester and Birmingham are steam mill mad. I don't mean to hurry you but I think…we should determine to take out a patent for certain methods of producing rotative motion from…the fire engine.' Demand from the mines for machines was drying up, and Boulton, the consummate entrepreneur, knew that the big market was in driving mills.

It took Watt three years of intense thought and experimentation to come up with the solution, his 'parallel motion' rotative engine, which he patented in 1784. The previous year Samuel Wyatt, the architect of the Albion Mill for grinding corn, which was being built in London by Blackfriars Bridge, had seen the new engine and ordered one on the spot. By 1786 it was powering six corn-grinding stones, and attracted many admiring visitors. Sadly, in 1791, the Albion Mill was completely destroyed by fire, but it had at least served to put on public display Boulton & Watt's new engine.

The first order for it from a textile mill came in 1785 from the cotton-spinning firm of Robinsons, in Popplewick, near Nottingham, who bought it as a reserve source of power. (It was there for emergencies when the water supply of the mills ran low.) The Robinsons had seven mills driven by water from the river Leen, the flow carefully controlled with dams and aqueducts. A problem arose when their neighbour, Lord Byron, began to construct ornamental ponds on his estate at Newstead Priory for mock sea battles he played with his servants. In order to do so, he allegedly tapped off the Robinsons' water supply and played havoc with

Opposite: From 1786, Jedediah Strutt began building water-powered cotton mills at Belper in Derbyshire. This cross-section of one of them illustrates the way in which a system of gearing from the mill-wheel turned hundreds of spindles and other mechanisms that transformed raw cotton into thread.

Printing calico cloth at the giant Swainson & Birley Cotton Mill near Preston in Lancashire around the 1840s. Of minor importance a century earlier, cotton manufacture became the single most important industry driving the first Industrial Revolution.

their mills. A legal dispute arose, and, in the meantime, the Boulton & Watt engine was laboriously assembled and put to work. But, as soon as they had won their battle with Byron, the Robinsons went back to water power.

It was not easy to set up a Boulton & Watt engine. It was very difficult to get the parts made and transported, an engineer had to be employed to fit the parts together, and the purchaser had to pay a patent fee. Progress was slow at first, but by 1800 there were more than 300 of the new rotary engines driving machinery, much of it in textile mills. The Boulton & Watt engine freed the textile mills from river power, and Richard Arkwright and others could start building them in Manchester, which would become Britain's cotton capital.

COTTON AND SLAVERY

All the developments to date of the Industrial Revolution – the smelting of iron with fuel other than charcoal, the mass-production of boilers in Coalbrookdale, the mechanisation of spinning, and the growth of overseas trade – now converged on Britain's newest industry, the production of cotton thread and cloth. From the very beginning it not only satisfied a home demand for light fabrics – what Defoe disparagingly called the 'new draperies' – but began to grow in importance for exports. In 1784–6 woollens had made up a quarter of all cloth sent abroad, and cotton only 6 per cent. By 1834–6, nearly half of all cloth exports were cotton, and woollens had fallen to 15 per cent. To begin with, most of this huge output went to Europe, the United States and Australia, but Africa and India were to become the biggest markets for British cottons.

By 1800 there was a huge demand for raw cotton. India could not supply it as the staple (fibre) used for their hand-spinning was not suitable for the new machinery. There would have been a severe check on the growth of the new industry had it not been for the chance visit of a young Yale graduate, Eli Whitney, to a plantation in South Carolina in 1793. One of the crops grown was a short-staple 'upland' cotton, coarser than the fine 'sea-island' cotton grown in the West Indies and on the coasts of the Carolinas and Virginia, but ideal for machine work. Whitney, noticing that production was seriously slowed down by the time it took one man or woman to separate the seeds in the cotton boll from the fibres, devised a rotating machine with teeth, rather like a hand-held circular cheese-grater, that did the job in a tenth of the time.

> In about ten days I made a little model, for which I was offered, if I would give up all right and title to it, a hundred guineas… I decided to turn my attention to perfecting the machine. I made one before I came away which required the labour of one man to turn it… And with which one man will clean ten times as much cotton as he can do in any other way before known; and also clean it much better than in the usual mode. And one man & a horse will do more than 50 men with the old machines. It makes the labour 50 times less without throwing any class of people out of business.

His cotton 'gin' (short for 'engine') revolutionised cotton production in the southern states of the newly independent USA.

When Whitney arrived, slavery had been on the way out: in fact, the Union voted to ban the Africa trade by 1808. Thanks to his invention, however, slaves

One simple machine transformed cotton production in the southern states of America, revived slavery and provided the new British mills with nearly all the raw material they needed. Eli Whitney's cotton 'gin', or engine, separated the cotton seeds from the fibres.

once again became valuable as toilers in the cotton fields, and their numbers rose throughout the southern cotton-growing region. Virginia, where cotton did not grow very well, specialised in supplying slaves to the states further south. To meet the demand, New England sea captains continued the African slave trade illegally.

English mills became totally dependent on slave-grown cotton. As the philosopher John Stuart Mill wrote in 1861, when he became editor of the *Richmond Examiner* in Virginia, and saw at first hand the auction of slaves like so many cattle: 'at the dawn of a hope that the demon [slavery] might now at last be chained and flung into the pit, England stepped in, and, for the sake of cotton, made Satan victorious'.

Nobody could deny that the single most significant industry created by the Industrial Revolution was absolutely dependent on a form of human bondage that the British themselves had outlawed. Karl Marx put it succinctly in a letter written in 1846:

> Direct slavery is as much the pivot of our industry today as machinery, credit, etc. Without slavery, no cotton; without cotton, no modern industry. It is slavery which has made the colonies valuable; the colonies have created world trade; world trade is the necessary condition of large-scale machine industry. Thus, before the traffic in Negroes began, the colonies supplied the Old World with only a few products and made no visible change in the face of the earth. Slavery is therefore an economic category of the highest importance.

The economic fortunes of Britain had turned full circle: Abraham Darby had experimented with iron-founding on the back of profits from the Bristol slave trade. With his coking system, he had laid the ground for a huge increase in the demand for coal to fuel steam engines, which the new ironworks could produce in quantity. In time, this gave rise to the dark, satanic mills of Lancashire, which then came to rely for their raw material – 90 per cent of cotton by the 1840s – on a revival of slavery in the former British colonies in America. And the end-product was a world clothed in wonderful cotton goods: cheap, lightweight and much more comfortable and easily washable than all but the finest woollens, almost like an ersatz silk for the masses. Of cotton garments, academic Douglas Farnie, in his 1979 classic *The Cotton Industry and the World Market 1815–1896*, says:

> They served as a symbol of civilisation and conferred status upon their wearers by associating them with the representatives of the greatest

imperial power of the century… Clothing also served as a token of acceptance of the Christian faith and as a quasi-sacramental manifestation of the inward and spiritual grace distinguishing one's brethren in Christ from 'naked savages'.

Among the many cotton items popular on the home market were cheap tea towels. These had originally been woven from linen, embroidered by servants, but kept by the mistress of the house for cleaning her precious china teacups. Now even the humble cottager had a tea towel, adding a small cost to the business of the daily brew.

This illustration, showing dresses made of the newest fabric – cotton – appeared in The Gallery of Fashion, *a magazine produced between 1794 and 1803, which was entirely devoted to the latest trends in clothing.*

EXPLORATION AND INDUSTRY

The speculative shipping of a cargo of calicos by the East India Company had been the first stimulus to create perhaps the most important manufacture of the Industrial Revolution. Britain's domination of world shipping then opened up new export markets, and exploration became a serious matter of State. However, there was still one vast portion of the world that had not been mapped, and there was a firm belief among some eminent scientists in England that the continent in question would yield untold riches. This territory, first imagined by the Greeks, was called *Terra Australis Incognita* or the Great Southern Continent. Remarkably, as late as the 1760s, the English geographer and fellow of the Royal Society Alexander Dalrymple was convinced that this southern continent was a reality. He had put together all the observations of expeditions that had explored the nether regions of the southern seas, which suggested that some fruitful land was just over the horizon, and added to this some spurious logic about the balance of the planet requiring there to be something really useful on its underside.

Dalrymple, from a distinguished Scottish family, had done a bit of seafaring, and though he was not a qualified seaman, fancied himself as the captain of a ship. It had not been uncommon for scientific voyages to be under the command of a man who had no experience at all as a mariner, just as English test cricket teams were once captained by 'gentlemen' who could barely hit a ball. When the Lords of the Admiralty decided to put up an expedition to the South Seas, and the Royal Society asked for it to include observation of an astronomical phenomenon known as the Transit of Venus, Dalrymple regarded himself as the ideal man to captain the ship. It would be launched in 1769, and, when the astronomical work was done, he could set sail for his imagined southern continent and claim its riches for Britain, beating such rivals as the French and the Dutch.

The Admiralty, however, flatly refused to put Dalrymple in charge. Instead they chose a navy man whom he, and most other scientists, had never heard of – James Cook. The appointment of this very competent, but relatively obscure, seaman was a clear indication that the Admiralty wanted professionals in charge of its expedition ships. Cook, however, did not come from a seafaring family. He was born the son of a farm labourer in Marton-in-Cleveland, a village near Middlesbrough, in 1728, and had started his working life in the picturesque Yorkshire fishing village of Staithes, not on the boats that crammed its tiny harbour, but in a grocery and draper's shop. James's father, who himself rose to be a farm manager, recognised his son had a good head for mathematics, and that shopkeeping would take him a rung up the social ladder.

However, when James was nearly eighteen years old he decided that he would try to get a job as an apprentice seaman. In the bustling port of Whitby, just down the coast from Staithes, he had seen the lines of 'cats' – collier ships that carried the coal from the north-east to London, and sometimes as far away as the Baltic – and fancied the idea of life aboard. He was really much too old to be apprenticed: most of the Whitby lads were taken on at the age of thirteen or fourteen. But James was persistent and impressed two Quaker brothers, John and Henry Walker, who owned collier ships, to take him on. He first sailed on a Whitby coal boat, the *Freelove*, as one of six apprentices. He stayed with the Walkers until he was twenty-seven, when they offered him the chance to become a captain. Instead, much to the dismay of some of his fellow sailors, he joined the navy, attracted by the fighting ships he had seen at Chatham dockyard when tacking up the Thames with a cargo of Newcastle coal.

Cook had learnt his seamanship on the treacherous North Sea coal run. In the navy he learnt mapping and surveying, honing his new skills in Newfoundland on the St Lawrence. When the Admiralty was looking for a captain for their South Seas expedition, he was forty-one. He could have had a choice of ships from Chatham, but he argued that the most suitable vessel for a two-year, round-the-world voyage carrying a party of scientists and their equipment, would be the kind of Whitby collier in which he had learnt his trade. The cats were not the finest-looking ships on the sea, but he knew how to handle them, they had been designed to sail in shallow waters and, as cargo boats, they had capacious holds. Cook got his way and chose the *Earl of Pembroke*, which was refitted, armed and re-named HMS *Endeavour*.

The coal trade had provided the expedition with both a ship and a captain. Government concern about the cost of importing into Britain such costly goods as Chinese tea and cotton grown outside the Empire now provided the *Endeavour* with the services of a man who was to advise governments over many years on the collection of botanic specimens: Joseph Banks. Born in 1743 into a well-to-do Lincolnshire family, Banks was much younger than Cook, and much wealthier, enjoying a tax-free private income of £6000 a year. He had many interests, but his chief love was botany, not so much out of idle curiosity, as from the belief that judicious planting of raw materials in territory Britain already 'owned' could greatly benefit the balance of payments. Following the successful *Endeavour* expedition, Banks became the toast of London, and was eventually elected president of the Royal Society. He also oversaw the collection of exotic plants kept at Kew Gardens, which grew from 600 specimens at the time of the expedition to 11,000 in 1813.

REVOLUTION AT SEA

The principal purpose of the *Endeavour* expedition was to observe an astronomical event – the transit of the planet Venus across the sun – that was predicted to occur on 3 June 1769. The ship left London on 21 July 1768 and sailed south, rounding Cape Horn on the tip of South America in January. By April it reached Tahiti, which scientists had calculated to be the best place for the observation. The seventeenth-century astronomer Edmund Halley had theorised that from this rare, but predictable, event it would be possible to calculate the distance between the Earth and the sun. This measurement would, in turn, provide the Astronomical Unit, which would allow the true scale of the universe to be calculated. The last transit had occurred in 1761, exactly as Halley had predicted, but after 1769 it would not occur again for a hundred years (the next one is in June 2004). So this was the last chance for eighteenth-century astronomers to crack what they regarded as the biggest problem they faced, the value of the Astronomical Unit.

Cook's expedition, like all the others that were observing the transit from different points around the Earth, had first to establish what line of longitude they were on for their observations to be valid. This required them to know what the local time was in order to be able to calculate their distance from Greenwich. Finding latitude on a ship at sea (how far north or south it had sailed) could be readily calculated by observations of the sun. But finding how far east or west it had gone was not so easy. It was known that for every 15 degrees of longitude travelling eastwards, local time moved ahead one hour from Greenwich meantime; the same distance travelling west moved local time one hour back. When, in 1714, a Board of Longitude was set up to encourage the invention of some means of calculating times at sea, a massive prize of £20,000 was offered to anyone who found the solution. But the terms set out were tough: the winner had to have a method that found longitude within half a degree (two minutes in time) and was of practical use at sea. It was well known that a clock that kept accurate time at sea would solve the problem of calculating longitude, but nobody believed the technology was there to make it. Meanwhile, an alternative method of navigating was provided by an almanac of 'lunar tables', which allowed longitude to be calculated according to the position of the moon.

Among those who set their sights on the prize was a Lincolnshire carpenter, John Harrison. He was born in 1693 and still a young man when the Board of Longitude first offered its reward. At the time he was making clocks entirely of wood, and even designed one that required no oil for its moving parts. It was not until 1730 that he put his mind, and considerable craftsman's skill, to the problem of a 'longitude' clock. He had to come up with an entirely new kind of mechanism

Opposite: The remarkable watchmaker John Harrison, looking proud and defiant. Harrison spent forty years of his life in a bid to win the Longitude Prize with a watch that would keep accurate time at sea. His 'chronometers' were beautifully crafted, but too expensive to go into immediate production, and it was some time after his death in 1780 that sea-clocks were in general use.

because the pendulum clock would never be any use on a ship tossed around at sea or subjected to sudden changes in temperature.

Harrison began by making spring-loaded clocks, which were essentially metal versions of his wooden mechanisms. These got nowhere near the accuracy required by the Board of Longitude, but he pressed on and developed H1, a clock that performed well enough on a voyage to Lisbon to give him hope that he was on the right track. For nearly twenty years, from 1740 to 1759, he experimented with a variety of devices that counteracted the expansion and contraction caused by temperature fluctuations. But the clocks that came of this, H2 and H3, failed the longitude accuracy test.

Now working with his son William, Harrison did not give up. In fact, he designed a completely new clock, about the size of a present-day alarm clock. When William took H4 on a run to Jamaica, it passed the accuracy test with flying colours. Harrison claimed his prize, but the Board of Longitude would not pay the full amount. The Board had been paying him expenses since 1737, sums between £15 and £1500. On the advice of the new Astronomer Royal, Nevil Maskelyne, they paid £3000 to the widow of Tobias Mayer, the man who had devised the lunar tables. Although they were tedious to use, the tables made it possible to calculate longitude at sea to an accuracy of half a degree.

Harrison was furious, and even more put out when, to claim his prize, he was asked to hand over all his blueprints and demonstrate that H4 was not a fluke and could be replicated. He and William were still wrangling with the Board when the *Endeavour* set sail in 1768, so James Cook missed the first opportunity he might have had to benefit from the revolutionary device. Nevertheless, Cook was such a gifted and meticulous seaman that he flawlessly navigated his expedition across the southern oceans, mapping as he went and providing the first outline of New Zealand.

Cook took a model of H4 on his second world tour, which set out in the *Resolution* in 1772, and paid tribute to its accuracy and value, describing it as his 'faithful guide through all the vicissitudes of weather'. (This was one of three made by Larcum Kendall. K1 went with Cook in 1772 and K2 was used by Captain Bligh on the *Bounty*. Kendall's K3 was a relatively cheap version, but, at 100 guineas, was still beyond the pocket of most sea captains. The equivalent price today would be more than £6000.) Eventually, in 1773, Harrison was paid £8750 by Parliament after representations from George III, who thought the inventor had been badly treated by the Board of Longitude. In all, by 1773, he had received a grand total in Board and Parliamentary payments of £23,065 – rather more than the original prize. He lived for another three years, dying at the age of 83, just as the *Resolution* returned in triumph. There is no doubt that the reluctance of the

Board of Longitude to award Harrison the prize was due to scientific snobbery – he was just a craftsman.

The dogged determination of John Harrison and his eventual success is an incredible story, first documented by Samuel Smiles in *Men of Invention and Industry* (1884), and more fully in 1923 by a naval officer called Rupert Gould, who had to leave active service after a mental breakdown and was put to work in the navy's Hydrographic Office. He found Harrison's clocks, which had been badly neglected, and documented their history in *John Harrison and His Timekeepers* (1987). More recently, the journalist Dava Sobel rescued Harrison once again from oblivion with her romantic account of his life's work in her book *Longitude* (1995).

However, the idea that Harrison was a 'lone genius who solved the greatest scientific problem of the age' and enabled Britain to dominate the high seas and build an Empire greatly exaggerates the significance of his clock. In the year Harrison died, Britain was defeated in the American War of Independence and lost the most valuable part of its Empire – the thirteen counties (as the British colonies were then called) populated by hundreds of thousands who had found their way across the Atlantic without a clock. In addition, Harrison's clock or chronometer was not easily replicated: to be of practical value it had to be much cheaper and mass-produced. As Dava Sobel points out, this required further invention before it became a standard item of navigational equipment at sea, and it was not widely used until after the 1820s. When he was shot at Trafalgar in 1805, Lord Nelson had a little pocket chronometer made by Josiah Emery, but it is not thought he used it for navigation. Such objects were fashionable pocket watches at the time.

Nevertheless, Harrison was a prime example of the extraordinary creativity of the Industrial Revolution. He was never a scientist, always a craftsman, largely self-taught and driven to solve a practical problem. The mechanisms he devised for the failed H3 clock – the enclosed bearings and the bimetallic strip – are used in many machines even today. In the nineteenth century the chronometer was invaluable for mapping and astronomical observation, and was used extensively when the next Transit of Venus occurred in 1869, though it once again proved impossible to calculate the Astronomical Unit.

Cook's second voyage on the *Resolution* finally put an end to Dalrymple's theory about the existence of a bountiful lost continent, but the fact that *Terra Australis* turned out to be an entirely uninhabited frozen waste was compensated for by the realisation that the marine life of the Antarctic seas was incredibly rich. When Australia was settled by the British in 1788, one of the first industries established was whaling, which provided much-needed oil for the street lamps of London and other big cities, and for the new engines of the Industrial Revolution.

FRANCE MARITIME.

Although the great voyages of Captain James Cook proved that there was no rich Terra Australis *beyond the southern oceans, the seas around Antarctica abounded in whales. These became highly valued for their oil, which was used in street lighting.*

Joseph Banks did not sail with the *Resolution*, but he became an adviser to many other expeditions, and a staunch advocate of growing cotton in the West Indies (before American cotton became available) and tea in India. It was not until after his death in 1820, however, that tea-planting in India freed Britain from its reliance on supplies from China.

TEATIME FOR THE MASSES

By the time Indian tea became the beverage of choice in Britain, a Quaker minister and apothecary had discovered the secret of making the most expensive element of the eighteenth-century tea ritual – the crockery. For centuries nobody in Europe had been able to work out how the Chinese made their delicate yet immensely tough porcelain. There were many theories about the ingredients of the clay from which it was made, but they all proved useless. A chemist working for King Augustus of Saxony (now part of east central Germany) was the first European to crack the formula, and small amounts of porcelain were made as early as 1710. But the King jealously guarded the secret.

In England a kind of porcelain was made in Bow, east London, in 1744, and the famous Royal Worcester pottery produced something similar in 1751. Although this was popular and went into mass production, the mixture of clays and ground stone was different from the kaolin mixture discovered in Saxony and used by tradition in China. So too were the methods of firing the pieces. The English imitations were made of what is technically called 'soft paste' porcelain, sometimes made using powdered glass rather than kaolin. All over Europe, potters, chemists and others who believed they could make a fortune continued to search for the magic Chinese formula for true porcelain.

The man who made the breakthrough was William Cookworthy, a weaver's son, born in 1705 in Kingsbridge, not far from the Devon seaport of Plymouth. A bright lad, William went to local schools and might have gone on to university had his family not suffered two disasters in succession when he was just a teenager. In 1718 his father died, and two years later his mother lost all their hard-earned investments in the collapse of the South Sea Company. At the age of fifteen William left school and was offered a position with Timothy and Sylvanus Bevan, Quaker apothecaries, who had recently moved from Wales to London, where they had set up the Plough Court Pharmacy. William had no money for a horse or the coach fare from Plymouth, so he walked the 240 miles to the capital. After five years living with the Bevan family, they set him up as a partner in Plymouth, and at the age of twenty he was in charge of Bevan & Cookworthy, dispensing chemists in Notte Street. In those days, and for long afterwards, chemists mixed their own potions, and were familiar with the chemical reactions of different powders.

A younger brother, Philip, went to sea as an apprentice on an East Indiaman, and brought back some Chinese porcelain, which William admired. But he was not a potter and had no thought then about trying to produce the ceramic himself. His great enthusiasm, once the chemist shop was well established, with two brothers as assistants, was preaching. In Plymouth he became well known, and was often visited by naval officers and travellers whose ships were harboured in the port. He also read avidly in French as well as English.

In 1736 a paper was published, originally in French, but later translated, which claimed to give an account of the way the Chinese made porcelain. A Jesuit priest, Père d'Entrecolles, working as a missionary in King-te-Ching had questioned local people about the materials used and got hold of some samples. He sent the key ingredients, called petuntse and kaolin by the Chinese, to a friend in France, and they were identified in a paper called *A Description of the Empire of China and of Chinese Tartary*, written by another Frenchman called Jean-Baptiste du Halde. Exactly when William Cookworthy came across this information is not clear, but it was certainly before 1744. In that year, by which time William was married with young children, he was visited by André Duche, an American of French Huguenot origin, who had crossed the Atlantic with a rather startling find for which he wanted an English market. A potter who lived in Savannah, Georgia, Duche had read du Halde's paper and recognised instantly that the Chinese petuntse and kaolin both occurred locally, and therefore bought land from the Native Americans with the idea of using it himself and exporting the surplus. When he visited Cookworthy, he brought samples with him.

For a brief period, Cookworthy went into partnership to open a pottery in Bristol, which would attempt to make a kind of porcelain with Duche's materials, but it seems to have come to nothing. What he really wanted was to find local supplies, and he was convinced that they must be in the mining regions of Devon and Cornwall if only he could identify them. During one of his explorations,

One of the earliest genuine English porcelain teacups made by William Cookworthy at his Bristol factory around 1768–70. Gilt edged and with a floral decoration, it is just possible that Captain James Cook sipped from a cup like this before setting off from Plymouth on the Endeavour *in 1768.*

around 1750, he stayed with the manager of the Great Work tin mine and had a look at the newly delivered Newcomen engine that had been installed to work winding gear and for pumping. He noticed the firemen re-lining the boiler and asked what they were using. It was a local clay called 'pot growan'. Cookworthy had seen it before, used as a mould by bell-makers and for oven bricks. He was sure it was kaolin, and collected a bagful of samples. On the same trip he found that common moorstone was very like the Chinese petuntse. Eventually, these key ingredients would become familiar as China clay and China stone.

Cookworthy's first attempts to fuse the two ingredients together were not very successful, and the death of his wife in the same year pushed his experiments aside. It was a long time before he was ready to take out a patent and begin a commercial porcelain works. This he finally managed in 1768, and he was busy putting the business together when the *Endeavour* called at Plymouth. He knew Captain James Cook, and invited him and Joseph Banks to dinner before they set sail for the South Seas. No doubt all three enjoyed a pot of tea, served perhaps in England's first home-produced porcelain cups.

CHAPTER TWO

New Lives, New Landscapes

On his tour of northern England in 1725, Daniel Defoe travelled from Nottingham to Derby, which he found 'a fine, beautiful and pleasant town'. He enjoyed the company of 'gentlemen' who preferred to live in the city than on their estates, which were mostly in the wilds of the Peak District. Always in search of novelty, Defoe was very eager to visit Derby's pride and joy, their latest piece of industrial machinery. 'Here is a curiosity in trade worth observing,' Defoe wrote in *A Tour Through the Whole Island of Great Britain* (1724–6), 'as being the only one of its kind in England, namely a throwing or throwster's mill.'

This was the Derby Silk Mill, built on the river Derwent around 1717, for the brothers John and Thomas Lombe. It was said that John had taken a job at a mill in Piedmont in northern Italy, and secretly made notes on how to construct the machinery that spun a fine thread. The brothers Lombe then took on a precocious local inventor, George Sorocold, who, as a teenager, had devised a mill that pumped water to houses in Derby. For the silk mill, Sorocold invented a wheel that rose and fell with the level of the river and turned the 'throwing' mechanism by a series of gears. Defoe was amused by the story that while showing visitors around, Sorocold had once slipped and fallen into the wheel, which spun him round and 'like Jonah's whale, spewed him out'.

Watermills were not, of course, a novelty for Defoe: he saw them everywhere he went on his tours. They ground corn, worked the bellows for foundries and powered all manner of machinery. What was novel about the Derby Silk Mill was that it was a kind of textile factory at a time when the preparation, spinning and weaving of wool, linen and a little cotton was everywhere a cottage industry. Women, children and old folk prepared and spun the thread, and men wove it. It

Before the invention of spinning machines and mill factories, the preparation of fibres to be made into thread was a cottage industry employing all members of the family. This family is preparing flax to make linen.

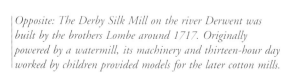

Opposite: The Derby Silk Mill on the river Derwent was built by the brothers Lombe around 1717. Originally powered by a watermill, its machinery and thirteen-hour day worked by children provided models for the later cotton mills.

was work that could be fitted into all the other activities of the day. Although families often worked for masters who provided the raw material and sold the finished cloth, their hours were not regulated, except by their need to earn money.

Defoe had seen this first hand in the hills around Halifax in Yorkshire. Everywhere he looked were little houses with, outside in the breeze, white pieces of cloth stretched on tenter frames to dry.

> Among the manufacturer's houses are…scattered an infinite number of cottages or small dwellings, in which dwell the workmen which are employed, the women and children of whom, are always busy carding, spinning etc so that no hand being unemployed, all can gain their bread, even from the youngest to the ancient; hardly any thing above four years old, but its hands are sufficient to itself.

There appeared to be nobody wandering around in the streets, but when Defoe knocked on the doors of the master manufacturers he saw 'a house full of lusty fellows, some at the dye-fat, some dressing the cloths, some in the loom, some one thing, some another, all hard at work'.

Three years after he wrote this, Daniel Defoe, a butcher's son who had made a name for himself (he added the De to his father's name of Foe), went into hiding to escape a creditor, and he died in 1731 without a penny to his name. But he left an invaluable record of Britain on the eve of a great upheaval that was to transform both the landscape through which he had travelled, as well as the working lives of those whose quiet industry had so impressed him. What Defoe did not do, according to his account, was look *inside* the Derby Silk Mill, for he would have seen there an image of the future: small children, some with platforms attached to their feet so that they could reach machinery, working a thirteen-hour shift.

As it happened, the first 'industrial village' that was the model for the future of the textile industry was built fifty years later on the river Derwent, not far from the Derby Silk Mill that had so intrigued Defoe. This was Cromford Mill, a wonder of the age, which made fortunes for the men who created it and, as its success was copied, turned cottagers into factory workers over a large part of northern England and southern Scotland.

Although, to those who first saw it, this new, water-powered spinning mill appeared to have sprung from nowhere in the wilds of Derbyshire, its creation can be traced back many years: in fact, the design of the Derby Silk Mill, still operating when Cromford Mill was built, was influential. The 'throwing' of silk was mechanised before the spinning of cotton, and there were already six silk mills operating when Cromford was built. The silk industry, however, operated on a much smaller scale.

The man whose vision created Cromford Mill was Richard Arkwright, born in Preston in December 1732, the youngest surviving son of a large and moderately well-off family. Not much is known about Arkwright's childhood, but it is thought he went to night school in Preston during the winter, and that a relative taught him to read. As a teenager, he was apprenticed to a barber-surgeon in Kirkham, near Preston, then moved on to Bolton, a town well known for producing fustian,

Sir Richard Arkwright, the former barber-surgeon and wig-maker, drew on the talents and inventions of others to create the 'water-frame', which revolutionised the preparation and spinning of cotton and made him a fortune.

55

a kind of coarse velveteen cloth made from a mixture of cotton and linen. (The term 'fustian', derived from the suburb of Fustat in Cairo, where it originated, came to mean pretentious or pompous.) Richard Arkwright was not then attracted to the fustian cottage industry, but was taken on by a wig-maker. A reminiscence of him during the eighteen years he stayed in Bolton as a wig-maker and part-time barber-surgeon suggests that he was modestly well-off, and known for his interest in mechanics (he had a clock in his wig shop that appeared to be driven by smoke from the chimney). He was thought 'very capital in bleeding and tooth-drawing'.

In 1755 Arkwright married Patience Holt, daughter of a schoolmaster, and they had a son, also Richard, born the same year. Sadly, Patience died in 1756, and Arkwright re-married in 1761. A year later he became a publican, while keeping on his wig-making business and working as a barber-surgeon. His time as a landlord lasted only two years, and he began to travel around Bolton collecting women's hair for his wigs while an assistant stayed in the shop. Exactly when, how and why he became interested in cotton-spinning is the subject of a hundred fanciful tales: one of the nicest is that he learned about Chinese methods of spinning from a sailor he met in a barber's shop, who regaled him with tales of his travels. What is known is that he got in with a number of different inventors, one of whom was supposedly trying to create a maritime clock to win the Longitude Prize, and that he began to examine the various efforts that had been made to create a mechanised spinning machine.

Spinning machines had already been made in the 1740s by a partnership between Lewis Paul, the son of a French refugee, and John Wyatt, a carpenter. They had gone as far as setting up donkey-powered mills to drive their machines, but they had failed to make a go of the business. This was partly because of technical problems, but also because they could not persuade enough people to turn up to work. Discipline, alongside technical and business skills, was the key to Arkwright's later success.

In the making of fustians, cotton was used only for the weft (horizontal threads) as it was not strong enough for the vertical threads of the warp, which were attached first to the weaver's frame. With the traditional forms of spinning-wheel (there were several different models) the correct tension to bind the cotton fibres together was applied by the practised hand of the spinner. To mimic that skill with a machine was not easy, and defeated many people. Paul and Wyatt had devised a system of rollers to hold the tension of the thread as it was spun from the loosely gathered strands of fibres called a 'roving'. A different method, using split hazel twigs, was used by James Hargreaves, who invented the hand-cranked spinning-jenny. Arkwright teamed up with a clockmaker in Preston in 1767 to

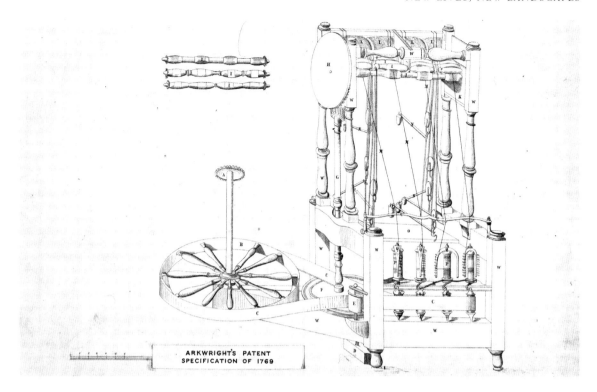

ARKWRIGHT'S PATENT
SPECIFICATION OF 1769

build a machine based on the Paul–Wyatt model, but modified so that it worked more efficiently.

The evolving model of the spinning machine was taken to Manchester and other places before Arkwright left Lancashire and went to Nottingham, home of the hosiery trade. Here he found business partners and considerable financial backing to set up a mill powered by 'gin' horses. This was not in operation when, through a Nottingham hosier, he was introduced to the forty-three-year-old Jedediah Strutt, owner of a silk-throwing mill in Derbyshire, and inventor of a knitting machine that made ribbed socks. Strutt took a look at Arkwright's 'frame' and suggested some alterations, but he was sufficiently impressed to go into business with him. In 1769 Arkwright and his partners applied for a patent for the spinning machine, supplying a detailed drawing of its working parts, which look like something devised by the cartoonist Heath Robinson: a tangle of pulleys and cogs driven by a belt, attached to a wheel which would be turned by eight horses, blinkered and circling dolefully for hours on end.

In the summer of 1771 Arkwright, Strutt and others with a financial interest in the project took a lease on a site next to the river Derwent, where a stream ran in from a nearby lead mine. The building of Cromford Mill began soon after. The river had provided energy for centuries: it powered corn mills, the bellows of an

The illustration that accompanied the first patent application by Richard Arkwright for his new spinning machinery, which was granted in 1769. The wheel was to have been turned by horsepower, but it was adapted to be driven by a mill-wheel on the river Derwent in Derbyshire, and the wheel became known as the 'water-frame'.

Cromford Mill on the river Derwent near Derby, built by Richard Arkwright and Jedediah Strutt in 1771. Such was the demand for cotton that the water-powered mill operated around the clock.

iron foundry, mills that pumped water from mines, and a paper-making mill, all nearby. Arkwright wanted a good flow of water that did not freeze in winter and this was provided by a stream or 'slough' from a mine. There was no village at the site, so housing was built for the families who would work here – pioneers of the new world of the factory.

The machinery housed in Cromford Mill was not the product of sudden inspiration, but sprang from years of experimentation with machine preparation and spinning of thread from raw materials: wool, silk, flax and cotton. Arkwright's water-frame, so called because it was driven by a mill-wheel, incorporated complex gearing and rolling mechanisms that could produce from cotton 'roving' a thread strong enough to be used for both warp and weft on a weaving frame. As Arkwright and Strutt were keen to point out, this meant that Britain could produce 100 per cent cotton cloth to compete with Indian fabric. And with ninety-six spindles whirring simultaneously in a purpose-built factory, they could spin thread in huge quantities and at great speed. They could also compete on price, provided the wages of those who tended the machines were kept to a minimum.

From the very beginning, most of those who tended the spinning machines in the mill were women and children. There was a relatively small workforce of skilled men to tend the machinery and act as overseers, and the houses had lofts in which men not employed in the factory could weave. Strutt and Arkwright advertised for children aged seven and over, but said they preferred them from the age of ten. They were contracted labour – for one year – and were expected to work thirteen-hour shifts, which included a one-hour meal break taken in the mill.

To make the enterprise pay, and to compensate for times when flooding or drought held up production, the machinery was kept going round the clock. Children alternated between the day and night shifts six days a week. The majority of this captive workforce were young boys, as girls tended to stay at home caring for younger brothers and sisters while their mothers were at work. In 1790, when Arkwright and Strutt mills were filling the valleys of Derbyshire and other counties, John Byng (alias Viscount Townsend) described the evening change of shift at Cromford: 'I saw the workers issue forth at 7 o'clock, a wonderful crowd of young people…a new set then goes in for the night, for the mills never leave off working… These cotton mills, seven stories high, and fill'd with inhabitants, remind me of a first rate man of war; and when they are lighted up, on a dark night, look most luminously beautiful.'

Discipline was severe. Children were given incentives to work, little prizes, but these were forfeited if they broke any of the rules. A Factory Inquiry Commission was given a list of misdemeanours that were punished by forfeits in the early 1800s, when Strutt and Arkwright's empires had made them the biggest cotton-spinners in the country. These included 'throwing bobbins at people', 'throwing tea on Josh Bridworth', 'terrifying S. Pearson with her ugly face', 'being saucy with W. Winson' and 'putting Josh Haynes's dog into a bucket of hot water'. Girls were punished for such things as going off with soldiers, disappearing to Derby Fair and leaving machines dirty. Quite often children would run away, and, in hot pursuit of his contracted labour, Arkwright would put a 'Wanted' advertisement in the local paper for their return, just as the slave owners in the southern states of America (which, after 1800, provided all of Arkwright's cotton) appealed for the return of 'negro slaves'.

And yet, by common consent at the time, the Arkwright mills, which spread to Lancashire and Scotland, provided the most humane working conditions. What had been established at Cromford gave rise to a huge new industry that was to become, by the 1840s, arguably the single most valuable creation of the first half-century of the Industrial Revolution. Arkwright and Strutt had set the wheels rolling, not only with their inventiveness and management, but by getting the law that forbade the making of pure cotton cloth overturned. Although it was widely ignored, this protectionist legislation, brought in to safeguard the woollen and silk industries, threatened the whole enterprise. It was agreed that blue threads would be woven into English cotton cloth to distinguish it from illegal imports from India. Getting Cromford Mill going was a huge and expensive operation, and Arkwright fought hard to hang on to his patents. But there was no stopping the new industry.

CHILD LABOUR

Much smaller mills appeared on the banks of fast-flowing streams all over Lancashire, and in many of these were to be found the true horrors of the factory system, which troubled the conscience of the nation and led to countless official investigations. The readiest supply of children was orphans in the care of various parish authorities, who considered them a burden on the rates. The parishes had the right to dispose of the orphans for various kinds of work, such as chimney-sweeping, and the children were the ideal cheap labour for the cotton mills. Makeshift 'prentice houses' were knocked up as dormitories. Pauper children were sent to these by the cartload from all over the country, including London, and they had no protection until laws to control child employment were introduced in the early 1800s. Some of these pauper children gave evidence against their former employers when inquiries were held into the working conditions in the mills.

Robert Peel, whose fortune was made in cotton, backed a new law introduced in 1803 that limited the working day of children to twelve hours, and banned night work – they had to finish by 9 p.m. It also stipulated that part of their day should be spent on reading, writing and arithmetic, that they should have one new suit of clothing every year, and that boys and girls had to sleep in separate dormitories, no more than two children to a bed. Many factory owners complained that such conditions were far too lenient and would never work. At the time Peel estimated that 20,000 of the mill apprentices had been placed there by the Poor Law overseers of their parishes. In 1812 the trade in pauper children from London and other cities was stopped when a law was passed that forbade their employment more than 40 miles outside their parish.

Meanwhile, the water-driven spinning mills were producing a huge quantity of thread, giving more work to the weavers, who enjoyed a boom time. (While they had money, they could also keep their children from mill work.) But then, in the 1790s, the great difficulty of running spinning mills with steam engines was solved, and they could be built in towns away from the old power supply of rivers and streams. Soon afterwards, in the 1820s, the first power looms were introduced, and the weavers were rapidly thrown out of work. Family survival meant that their children had to work in the steam-driven mills.

By 1786, Richard Arkwright was a very rich man, who had bought up estates and was ready for some recognition of his services to the country. He was knighted by George III but, according to an account by a witness, Wilhemina Murray, 'the little great man had no idea of kneeling, but crimpt himself up in a very odd posture which I suppose His Majesty took for an easy one so never took the trouble to ask him to rise'. The following year, Sir Richard became the High

Sheriff of Derbyshire. In keeping with his elevated position in society, he began building a huge mansion, to be called Willersley Castle, on one of his estates. It was still being lavishly furnished and the gardens laid out when, in August 1791, it was badly damaged by fire. One year later Sir Richard died. In just twenty years, the Arkwright-Strutt partnership had transformed the working lives of hundreds of thousands and changed the landscape in mill country. Daniel Defoe would hardly have recognised the countryside around Derby, nor much of rural England, now cut through with canals, and with men at work reclaiming for agriculture and industry the wild heaths and marshes he had hurried past. In 1771, just as Cromford Mill was being built on the Derwent, the agricultural journalist Arthur Young wrote in *The Farmer's Tour through the East of England* that he was '...agreeably surprized to find the country from Derby to Matlock in general enclosed and cultivated. Derbyshire being generally reputed as waste a country as any in England; I was led to expect large tracts of uncultivated country in every quarter of it; but all the southern parts of it are rich: in this track are some un-enclosed commons, but they bear no proportion to the cultivated land.'

The horse-drawn seed-drill shown here was invented by Jethro Tull.

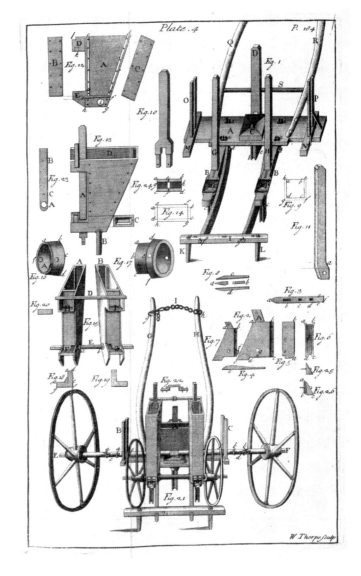

LAND ENCLOSURE

Young was at this time a great advocate of enclosure, which involved converting whole districts of small farms or heaths and bogs into larger fields, usually with a single owner intent on 'improving' the land by new methods of cultivation, such as Jethro Tull's horse-drawn plough and seed drill. Only on this newly fashioned farmland, so the advocates of enclosure argued, could more wheat and other crops required by the ever-rising population of the country be

61

This quaint image of eighteenth-century farm work in fact shows an innovation: the plough is drawn by horses instead of oxen, and is steered by just one ploughman. Ox-drawn ploughs needed a second man to lead the team, so the labour-saving horse plough was regarded as much more efficient.

grown. Arthur Young at first could think of nothing good to say about the old, fragmented, 'open field' farming, which was rapidly disappearing. Each year as much as a third of the land would lie fallow, producing nothing while it regained its fertility. There was little or no experimentation with new crops or the rotation system, and the heaths were left barren, used only as sources of firewood and for grazing skinny cattle and ragged sheep. Not everyone agreed with Young, and in his *Political Arithmetic* (1774) he raged against the opponents of improvement:

> What will these gentlemen say to the enclosures of Norfolk, Suffolk, Nottinghamshire, Derbyshire, Lincolnshire, Yorkshire, and all the northern counties? …What say they to the wolds of York and Lincoln, which from barren heaths, at 1s per acre, are BY ENCLOSURE alone rendered profitable farms? …How, in the name of common sense, were such improvements to be wrought by little or even moderate farmers? Can such enclose wastes at a vast expense – cover them with a hundred loads an acre of marl – or six or eight hundred bushels of lime…and conduct those mighty operations essential to new improvements? No. It is to the great farmers you owe these.

There was nothing essentially new about enclosure: it had been going on for many years, but at a slow pace, and often by agreement between owners of land and the commons on which a local community had rights of grazing and collecting firewood. It was the increasing use of Parliamentary enclosure, whereby the land transfer was brought about by a special Act, that caused fierce argument because this was, in effect, a form of compulsory purchase. Some would say daylight robbery because a commission would sit to hear the case of the various parties pleading the loss of their ancient rights, and promptly wipe them out. Parliament was, after all, composed chiefly of landowners, who were unlikely to legislate against their own interests.

The petitions presented to the House of Commons make for doleful reading. The following, for example, was submitted by the village of Raunds in Northamptonshire in June 1797:

> That the petitioners beg leave to represent to the House that, under pretence of improving lands in the said parish; the cottagers and other persons entitled to Right of Common on the lands intended to be inclosed, will be deprived of an inestimable privilege, which they now enjoy, of turning a certain number of their cows, calves and sheep, on and over said lands; a privilege that enables them not only to maintain themselves and their families in the depth of winter…

A vista of 'improved' farmland on the estate of Lord Thurlow in Surrey. The enclosure of common fields was bitterly opposed by villagers, who lost their livestock and were turned into paid labourers. But enclosure undoubtedly made farming more efficient.

This was at a time when the demands of war with France had hastened the process of enclosure, with high prices for wheat and a sustained demand for home-grown food, a circumstance not lost on the desperate villagers of Raunds.

> …a more ruinous effect of this inclosure will be the almost total depopulation of their town, now filled with bold and hardy husbandmen, from among whom…the nation has hitherto derived its greatest strength and glory, in the supply of its fleets and armies, and driving them, from necessity and want of employ, in vast crowds, to the manufacturing towns, where the very nature of their employment, over the loom or the forge, soon may waste their strength…

The rise of the factory system coincided in many regions with enclosure, and it appeared to those turned off the land that they were being forced from a way of life they were content with into a hell of machine-driven servitude. It was not, generally speaking, that there was less work about: the process of reclaiming land and re-organising the field system was labour intensive, and the vast increase in the output of thread and cloth that the factories brought about created more jobs than were lost. What changed fundamentally over a large part of Britain was a way of life in which cottagers who could once get by with a spinning-wheel, a weaving or knitting frame and a little livestock had either to become landless farmworkers or head for the manufacturing towns. At Cromford Mill, Arkwright had recognised the ingrained affection that country people had for their animals, and early on bought them milk cows that they could pasture close by.

Oliver Goldsmith, the Irish writer who had studied medicine in Edinburgh, travelled in Europe and generally led a poverty-stricken existence in England, wrote about the heart-rending changes that were visible everywhere in the countryside. His poem called simply *The Enclosures* (1770) makes the point:

> *Sweet smiling village, loveliest of the lawn,*
> *Thy sports are fled, and all thy charms withdrawn;*
> *Amidst thy bowers the tyrant's hand is seen,*
> *And Desolation saddens all thy green:*
>
> *…times are alter'd; Trade's unfeeling train*
> *Usurp the land, and dispossess the swain;*
> *…rural mirth and manners are no more.*

Goldsmith certainly romanticises 'rural mirth and manners', but even Arthur Young, the staunch promoter of enclosure, was shocked by its effects on country people. In 1801 he wrote *An Inquiry into the Propriety of Applying Wastes to the Better Maintenance and Support of the Poor* after investigating the social impact of enclosure over a wide area. He tried to get information on 140 Parliamentary enclosures, but could find what he needed to judge the effect on the poor in only thirty-seven cases. Of these, twenty-five had clearly 'injured' the rural poor, who were deprived of land and grazing rights, and had nowhere to keep even one cow. As a result, they became a charge on the parish poor rates. Although Young never lost his faith in enclosure brought about with the interests of the 'peasantry' in mind, he did rage against the impossible position the landless poor were in.

In the 1830s riots broke out in many counties where enclosure of land had deprived villagers of their grazing rights on common land.

Go to an alehouse kitchen of an old enclosed country, there you will see the origin of poverty and poor rates. For whom are they to be sober? For whom are they to save? (Such are their questions.) For the parish? If I am diligent, shall I have leave to build a cottage? If I am sober, shall I have land for a cow? If I am frugal, shall I have half an acre of potatoes? You offer not motives; you have nothing but a parish officer and a workhouse!
– Bring me another pot –

The social impact of enclosure was obviously most sharply felt in those parts of the country where there had been open fields and villages. When, in 1830, rioting broke out in the countryside, the counties most affected were Sussex, Hampshire, Kent, Suffolk, Norfolk, Berkshire, Buckinghamshire, Wiltshire, Oxfordshire, Northamptonshire, Huntingdonshire, Bedfordshire, Devon, Dorset, Gloucestershire and Cambridgeshire. Hayricks were burnt and threshing machines smashed by farm labourers, and farmers threatened in letters from a mysterious 'Captain Swing'. But the terrible hardships in England could not compare with the brutal eviction of the Scottish people from their homes during the first Highland clearances of the 1790s, as landowners sought to profit from raising sheep.

South of the border, the transformation of heath and bog into fertile land, a very expensive business, was a genuine improvement that caused less suffering than enclosure of old farmland. John Wilkinson, the celebrated ironmaster and maker of cannons, put a good deal of his fortune into reclaiming huge acres of estates he owned near Grange-over-Sands in Cumbria. To reclaim impoverished soils he mined clay and lime and spread it over the peat bogs, and eventually grew fodder

An early steam threshing machine, which brought industrialism to the farm. The ironmaster John Wilkinson was one of the first 'improvers' to use such a machine on his estates.

HORNSBY'S PORTABLE STEAM-ENGINE AND THRESHING MACHINE.—(SEE NEXT PAGE.)

The famous Soho manufactory built by Matthew Boulton on what had been heathland outside Birmingham. In this illustration the boilers for steam engines are being made. Boulton liked to say, 'We make here what all the world wants – power!'

crops, such as the pink-flowered sainfoin, sometimes called 'holy clover', which was popular for cattle feed. Wilkinson also introduced steam-driven corn-threshing machines to his Welsh estate.

In many places the heaths that were enclosed were regarded as the slums of the day on which the very poorest of the rural community eked out a meagre living. After enclosure they would move to jerry-built industrial towns. To build his Soho Works, Matthew Boulton acquired enclosed land, including part of a common. Writing to Lord Hawksbury many years later, he justified his creating wealth out of a desolate heath:

Matthew Boulton, one of the most inventive of all eighteenth-century manufacturers. Although chiefly known for his partnership with James Watt in producing an improved steam engine, Boulton made a great range of ornamental goods.

> …I founded my manufactory upon one of the most barren commons in England, where there existed a few miserable huts filled with idle niggardly people, who, by the help of the common land and a little thieving, made shift to live without working. The scene now is entirely changed. I have employed a thousand men, women and children, in my aforsaid manufactory, for nearly thirty years past.

Boulton, like Arkwright and Strutt before him, built himself a fine house, and had the gardens laid out, partly with the assistance of the great landscape architect Humphry Repton.

HIDDEN RICHES OF THE LAND

All this 'improvement' – the marking out of enclosed fields with their new boundaries (often hawthorn hedges), the draining of swampy land with newly devised clay and, later, iron pipes, the cutting of canals where the gradient of the ground was crucial – required expertise. Map-making became important in the surveying of estates, whether it was to decide where boundaries fell, or to show the layout of great gardens, or the route of a canal. The art of accurate measurement, judgement of scale, knowledge of underlying soils and so on were valued. And for any landowner jealous of the fortune a relative or neighbour had made from the chance discovery of coal on their estate, a surveyor claiming some special understanding of where this treasure might be found was as sought after as a physician who boasted the cure for disease.

Just as medical practice has an ancient history, so too has the science of exploring for valuable minerals. Professor Hugh Torrens, a geologist now retired from Keele University, has unearthed a number of very early works, including a German publication from 1500 on the search for 'vein' minerals. Unlike coal seams, these cut through strata, sometimes vertically. In 1672 George Sinclar, a Scottish philosopher, who was thrown out of Glasgow University and subsequently became an engineer and surveyor, included a chapter entitled 'A Short History of Coal' in his *magnum opus The Hydrostatics or…Fluid Bodies*. According to Sinclar, sharp observation was the key – studying the land, mapping it and picking up rocks from the ground. Boreholes were made and shafts cut into the layers of rock. In 1708 an anonymous publication from Newcastle-upon-Tyne, called *The Compleat Collier*, offered a way of 'discovering…where coal lies: and…preventing boring where coal is not'.

Methods of boring were unsophisticated, and a narrow rod passing through layers of rock might pass straight through a coal seam without showing any evidence in the murky material drawn back to the surface. In any case, there was still the problem of where to sink a borehole. There were no professional geologists as such, but the demand for coal inspired a number of men with an interest in rocks and fossils to offer ideas about where it might be found. The biographer John Aubrey completed a paper in 1673 that related the existence of subterranean minerals to the vegetation on the surface. Nearly forty years later a Cumbrian vicar, Thomas Robinson, published his theories on how to discover minerals, such as coal, in strata, as well as those occurring in veins. It is doubtful if they were ever of much practical use, and were certainly less sophisticated than the first really comprehensive account of rock formation by an extraordinary Scotsman, James Hutton, born in Edinburgh in 1726.

Hutton first studied law, then moved on to medicine and agriculture. While travelling in Europe, he began a private study of rock formations. He did not

James Hutton examining rock strata. Hutton was one of the first to propose that the creation of rock formations was dynamic, arising from upheavals in the Earth's crust. He has been called the 'father of geology' for his trail-blazing work, which was first published in 1785.

marry, but lived with his three sisters on the family farm in Berwickshire, and later in Edinburgh, where he wrote a paper presented to the newly formed Royal Society in Edinburgh in 1785. He called it *Theory of the Earth, or an Investigation of the Laws Observable in the Composition, Dissolution and Restoration of Land upon the Globe*. He noted that rocks decayed and formed other rocks, that upheavals in the Earth caused strata to bend, and that veins of minerals were forced into strata: in other words the creation of the Earth's crust was dynamic. Rather like those who panned for gold, he gathered samples of rock washed down by streams, searching for evidence of what might be found where the water cut through the strata. Professor Torrens notes that when Captain Cook set off on the *Endeavour* in 1768, he was advised by a friend of Hutton's to examine the gravel at the mouth of rivers as an indication of what minerals might lie inland.

Brilliant though Hutton's work was, it was not necessarily of practical value in finding coal where there was no surface indication that it might exist. Another well-meaning theorist, William Sharpe, a vicar and schoolmaster who moved from the coal-mining county of Durham to Dorset, offered a prospector's guide called *A Treatise upon Coal Mining or an Attempt to Show Marks and Indications* (1769). Because of the costs of transport, coal in Dorset was pricey, and poor people could not afford enough of it to keep warm. The Rev. Sharpe thought he could solve the problem by looking for telltale signs in the Dorset countryside, such as acid streams and the presence of ironstone or blue clay. Had he been proved correct, the landscape of that part of the West Country and the lives of those living there would have been transformed: the discovery of coal would give rise to a kind of instant industrialism, as the steam-powered pumping machines moved in, and the winding gear and miners' houses were thrown up.

As it turned out, the Rev. Sharpe's belief that where there was blue or black shale there was coal proved to be illusory. Boreholes costing thousands of pounds were sunk, and produced nothing, the work hampered by miners from the Mendip Hills, who feared for their livelihood and tried to sabotage the prospecting. The holes were narrow and could easily be jammed with an iron bar, or, more subtly, a piece of coal could be placed in them to encourage a fruitless search. Boring did not become a really useful form of prospecting until 1805, when an Irish canal surveyor, James Ryan, invented a cylindrical cutter, based on a trepanning saw used by surgeons to remove bone from the skull. This produced a neat core of rock that showed the sequence of strata, rather than a ground-up mass of different layers.

Alongside the search for new sources of raw materials, or reserves that were local and did not have to carry the cost of transport, there was the more genteel pursuit of fossil collecting. This was long before any formulations of evolutionary theory by Alfred Wallace and Charles Darwin would put the study of palaeontology at the centre of scientific debate. Fossils were interesting and charming in their own right, and it was not necessary to imagine that they were relics of the biblical flood that Noah had failed to haul on to the Ark to become a collector. The great increase in excavations of all kinds for clay and coal and canal construction increased the range and quantity of these petrified relics, and they were gathered and arranged by many enthusiasts.

One of these was William Smith, the son of the blacksmith at Churchill, an Oxfordshire village. Born in 1769, he left home at the age of eight, when his father died, to live with an uncle who was a farmer. He collected fossils as a boy, and his interest in the land led him to become a pupil of Edward Webb, a surveyor based at Stow-on-the-Wold in Gloucestershire, when he was eighteen. During the four years he worked for Webb, Smith took on a variety of work and travelled a good deal, noting the variations and continuities in rock structure, and the relationship between strata and particular kinds of fossil found in them. In his last year with Webb, 1791, he was sent to survey an estate in north Somerset that had coal mines, and whose owner was keen to find more deposits. Smith therefore gained early experience of coal prospecting, while adding to his collection of fossils and absorbing local knowledge of where they occurred, and in what sequence. He was to tell his nephew John Phillips:

> Fossils have been long studied as great curiosities, collected with great
> pains, treasured with great care and at great expense, and shown and
> admired with as much pleasure as a child's rattle or a hobby-horse is
> shown and admired…because it is pretty; and this has been done by
> thousands who have never paid the least regard to that wonderful order
> and regularity with which Nature has disposed of these singular
> productions, and assigned to each class its peculiar stratum.

By 1793, Smith had impressed local landowners enough to get the lucrative appointment of surveyor for a prospective new coal canal which would have to be cut along the sides of two valleys, and promised to be a mammoth engineering task. So that they could have the best advice possible, the investors in the canal sent Smith, along with two coal-mine owners, to look at the canals that had already been cut in the north of England. One of the innovations they came across was the concept of a 'caisson', which operated as a kind of hydraulic lift to carry barges over steep inclines. It looked like just the thing needed for one problematic section of the Somerset Canal, but it was to seal Smith's fate for many years. He was not to be the canal engineer, but became a promoter of the caisson, which was soon under construction and a wonder of new technology that attracted sightseers.

The cutting of the canals revealed a great deal about the sequence of rock beds, and Smith added to his collection of fossils, asking workmen cutting the canal to save them for him. He was secure in his job as surveyor, was elected to the Bath Agricultural Society in 1796, bought himself a 17-acre estate at Tucking Mill, close to the newly created canal, took on an assistant and began to write up his discoveries about the strata in the region, observing always the regular order they presented. He gave the layers numbers, working from the top down, beginning with 'The Chalk' and going down to layer twenty-three, 'The Coal'.

Smith at this time looked set fair to lead a comfortable life, combining his professional work as a surveyor with his own special interest in the sequence of strata and their associated fossils. He began to indicate these on geological maps of the Bath area. And, like many professionals in his day, thought he might prosper with a bit of free enterprise working the local Bath stone. But everything went wrong. His stone business failed and then, in 1799, during a period of exceptionally heavy rain, the caisson on the canal began to leak and was destroyed. It was a disaster for which Smith was not directly responsible, but he was fired. The deluge, however, gave him a new line of work: draining, and sometimes irrigating, farmland. He was saved from penury by the great movement for agricultural improvement, working for an impressive roll-call of aristocrats and gentry, including the Marquis of Bath and the Duke of Bedford. He worked everywhere, travelling, by his own estimation, thousands of miles a year. His understanding of rock strata was talked of in agricultural circles, and through his elevated social contacts he met the mighty Joseph Banks, who became something of a patron, encouraging Smith to publish his maps.

In 1800, Smith was just thirty years old, and yet his knowledge of the landscape of large parts of England, from Yorkshire to Dorset, gleaned on his never-ending round of work on large estates, was unparalleled. The following year, for the first time, he was asked to apply his knowledge not to improving farmland, but to finding coal beneath it. This was at Pucklechurch in Gloucestershire, where there was a coalfield close by. But nothing was found. Nor did Smith find coal on an estate east of Bath, where the boring hit water, which was pumped out with huge steam engines, which in turn began to drain the supply to Bath's popular and lucrative springs. He did not, of course, have a free hand in where he went prospecting for coal: he had to take commissions that came his way.

Despite these disappointments, what Smith had begun was a scientific approach to mineral exploration based on a detailed knowledge of how patterns of

POPULAR GEOLOGY.

EXPLANATION

The Diagram represents the order in which the different strata lie upon each other, this order is never inverted, although many groups may be absent, and in some districts one of the lowest systems may be found immediately below the surface.

FOSSILS	SUBDIVISIONS.	GROUPS OF STRATA, With their Average Thickness.		USES IN THE ARTS.	LOCALITIES.
		RECENT AND SURFACE SOIL.			
Extinct mammalia.	Crag.	PLIOCENE		Building, Agriculture	Norfolk.
Planorbis, Helix &c Tropical fruits, &c.	Isle of Wight Beds London Clay, &c.	EOCENE. 2,500 feet.		Glass making, &c. Building, Potteries.	Isle of Wight. London, &c.
Foraminifera, &c.	Chalk, Greensand.	CRETACEOUS. 1,400 feet.		Building, Rd. making	Kent, &c.
Iguanodon.	Clay, Sands, &c.	WEALDEN AND PURBECK.		Building, &c.	Kent, Sussex.
Ammonites, &c.	Up. M. Low. Oolites	OOLITES. 1,670 feet.		Building, Potteries.	Central England.
Great Saurians.	Shale & Limestone	LIAS. 800 feet.		Building, &c.	Leicestersh. &c.
Labyrinthodon.	Red Sandstone, &c.	TRIASSIC, or N. R. SANDSTONE.		Building, &c.	Cheshire, &c.
Productus, &c.	Mag. Limestone.	PERMIAN, 600 feet.		Used for H. of Parlmt	Sunderland, &c.
Fossil Plants, chiefly Ferns and Conifers; Insects.	Coal Measures, 3,000 to 10,000 feet. Millstone Grit, 600 feet.	CARBONIFEROUS.		The great sources of Coal, also iron ore and fire clay. Building, paving, and mill-stones.	Durham, South Wales, &c. Northern Counties, &c.
Marine Shells. Corals, Crinoids, Trilobites, Fish. Reptile: Archegosaurus.	Mountain Limestone, 500 to 1,400 feet. Limestone Shales, 1,000 feet.	5,000 to 13,000 feet.		Ornamental marbles. Chief sources of lead ore. Scotch coal, and iron stone.	Yorkshire, Derbyshire, &c. Lanarkshire.
Corals, Bryozoa, Brachiopods, Mollusca, Trilobites, Fish, and Reptiles.	Upper Devonian. Middle Devonian. Lower Devonian.	DEVONIAN. 5,000 to 8,000, feet.		Local building stone, flagstones and paving stones, roofing slates, &c.	N. Scotland, &c. Herefordshire&c Devonshire, &c.
Shells of every class, Brachiopoda most abundant; Corals, and Sauroid Fish.	Ludlow Rocks, 2,000 feet. Wenlock Rocks, 1,800 feet. Woolhope Series 3,050 feet.	UPPER SILURIAN. 6,850 feet.		Building materials. Building stones, lime, and flux for iron smelting.	Ludlow, &c. Wenlock-edge. Woolhope, &c.
Trilobites, as Calymene, Phacops, &c.	Llandovery Rocks, 2,000 feet.	MIDDLE SILURIAN. 2,000 feet.		Of little economic value.	Llandovery.
Crinoidea, Corals, Mollusca, chiefly Brachiopoda. Large Trilobites. Trinucleus ornatus Lingula Davisii. Olenus Micurus.	Caradoc and Bala Rocks, 8,000 feet. Llandeilo Rocks, 5,000 feet.	LOWER SILURIAN.		Good building stones, and roofing slates. Impure limestone for burning. Paving stones, road materials, and limestone for burning.	Caradoc. Bala, Horderley. Llandeilo. Builth.
Hymenocaris vermicauda. Agnostus pisiformis.	Lingula Flags, 4,000 feet.	17,000 feet.		The flagstones and traps are quarried for road stones, &c.	Tremadoc. Festiniog, &c.
The earliest traces of life occur in the Cambrian Strata, and comprise peculiar Algæ, Bryozoa, Brachiopoda, and Crustacea. Oldhamia radiata, O. Antiqua, Arenicolites didyma, Histioderma Hibernicum.	Longmynd and Cambrian Rocks.	CAMBRIAN. 20,000 feet.		The source of good roofing slates, slabs for cisterns, &c. Hones for cutlery	Harlech. Snowden. Cader Idris. Skiddaw. Cumberland. Anglesea, &c.
No Organic remains discovered in these Rocks.	Clay slate, Mica Schist. Gneiss and Quartz Rocks.	MICA SCHIST. GNEISS.		Roofing slates, plumbago, garnets, &c. Veins of copper, lead ore, &c.	Cumberland. Scotland, &c.
For further details see Morris's Geological Chart.	Granite, Syenite, &c.	GRANITE.		Bridges, paving, &c.	Devon, Aberdeen &c.

Vertical labels in strata column: SECONDARY. TERT. / PALÆOZOIC, or PRIMARY. / HYPOZOIC. / PLUTONIC. Total thickness numbers: 2,800 / 6,180 / 65,450 FEET.

(London, Impermeable Clay, Porous with Water, Chalk, Blue Clay)

The search for coal during the eighteenth century saw the dawning of a dynamic view of rock formation, and the beginning of scientific methods of mineral exploration. It was understood that strata had been laid down at different times in the Earth's history, and each of these was named – the coal-bearing seams being marked as 'carboniferous'.

rock strata are repeated, and with this knowledge he, and those who adopted his system, were able to say with considerable conviction where coal *would not be found* at a mineable depth. John Farey, who was trained by Smith, wrote in 1806:

> …almost every common, moor, heath or piece of bad land in parts where coals are scarce, have at one time or other been reported by ignorant coal finders to contain coal…our inquiries, and those of Mr Smith, have brought to light hundreds of instances, where borings and sinkings for coals have been undertaken…in southern and eastern parts of England, attended with heavy and sometimes almost ruinous expenses to the parties…

Those who profited, said Farey, were the men who set themselves up as coal prospectors, often returning to the same spot where their boreholes had revealed nothing the first time round. William Smith's meticulous study of the succession of rocks was therefore a threat to the livelihood of many. And those who took a more academic interest in the newly emerging study of geology did not necessarily accept his findings. When the Geological Society was formed in 1807, William Smith was not invited to become a member. The eminent scientist Humphry Davy was, and he doubted Smith's findings.

All this was put right later when a so-called 'Smith cult' arose and he was spoken of as the 'father of geology' and, in 1831, awarded the society's highest honour, the Woollaston Medal. But for a long time what he had understood, and would have been of great value in the search for coal and other valuable minerals, was not made use of. Smith's wonderful geological map, first published in 1815, was disregarded by those who imagined they might have coal on their estates. Indeed, his lack of success led him into financial difficulties, and in 1819 he was put into the King's Bench prison for debtors in London. The eventual change in his fortune saw him given a pension by William IV, and he retired to Scarborough in Yorkshire, where he built a rotunda to house his fossil collection, arranged in order of succession.

The demand for coal rose continually, and old mine workings were dug deeper as the seams were followed. Whereas the cotton mill factories were new, and working conditions attracted attention, coal-mining had gone on for centuries, and the plight of the pit workers, who included thousands of children, was largely ignored. Every year the death toll of miners rose. The mine owners regarded pit disasters as a normal hazard of the job, and in Northumberland and Durham there were usually no inquests into accidents. It was left to those who saw whole communities devastated to seek some way of making mines safer. In Sunderland a

Opposite: One of the earliest geological maps of England, Wales and part of Scotland, drawn in 1815 by William Smith and based on his extensive study of the variegated pattern of rock strata. Smith travelled the country as a surveyor, canal builder, fossil collector and mineral prospector, and the map represents his observations made over many years.

A
DELINEATION
OF THE
STRATA
OF
ENGLAND AND WALES,
WITH PART OF
SCOTLAND;
EXHIBITING
THE COLLIERIES AND MINES;
THE MARSHES AND FEN LANDS ORIGINALLY OVERFLOWED BY THE SEA;
AND THE
VARIETIES OF SOIL
ACCORDING TO THE VARIATIONS IN THE SUBSTRATA;
ILLUSTRATED BY THE MOST DESCRIPTIVE NAMES.
BY W. SMITH.

THE GERMAN OCEAN

THE IRISH SEA

ST. GEORGE'S CHANNEL

CARNARVON BAY

CARDIGAN BAY

BRISTOL CHANNEL

THE ENGLISH CHANNEL

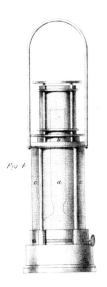

Until the invention of Davy's safety lamp, explosions in mines were common because the naked flames used to illuminate the pits often ignited the methane gas that accumulated under ground.

society was formed for the prevention of accidents, and they asked the leading 'gas' expert, Sir Humphry Davy, for help. After a visit to Newcastle-upon-Tyne, he set to work and devised a lamp with a metal gauze surround, which dispersed the heat of the flame so that it would not cause firedamp (methane) in the pits to explode. In the presence of an inflammable gas, the flame would glow a warning blue, and the 'safety lamp' could be used to detect carbon dioxide, which would put out its flame.

The first trials of the Davy lamp were in 1816. Davy could have patented the lamp (which would have caused a conflict with George Stephenson, who invented one at the same time), but he chose not to so that it could be quickly adopted in the mines. His heart was in the right place, but the effect of the Davy lamp was not what he had hoped for. Some mine owners saw it as a way of saving money by doing away with ventilation systems, and the safety lamp enabled them to send miners into deeper, hotter seams. Steam engines could pump water out from greater depths, though the technology of the coalfields remained incredibly primitive, with machinery operated by children. In 1842 the First Report of the Commission on the Employment of Children and Young Persons found that ventilation doors in mines, if left open, could save many lives, 'and yet, in all the coal mines, in all the districts of the United Kingdom, the care of these trap doors is entrusted to children of from five to seven or eight years of age, who, for the most part sit, excepting for a few moments when persons pass through these doors, for twelve hours consecutively in solitude, silence and darkness'.

POPULATION GROWTH

Despite the almost unimaginable hardships suffered by the first generations who lived through the first century of industrialisation, the population rose continuously. In England, at a rough estimate, there were just over 5 million people in 1701. The population was higher, but still under 6 million, when Daniel Defoe set out on his tours in the 1720s. By 1801, when the first national census was taken, it was 8.6 million, and it doubled again by 1851. Child mortality fell and then rose again in the insanitary conditions of many of the new industrial towns. The flight from the countryside to what William Cobbett called the 'wens' (warts), London being the 'Great Wen' on the landscape, was quite astonishing. In Defoe's England only about 15 per cent of the population lived in towns of 10,000 or more inhabitants. By 1800, as many more towns reached that size, they housed about a quarter of the population. And by 1840 England had become thoroughly urbanised, with nearly half the population in towns, and the majority of those living in rural areas landless labourers, earning a wage.

Below: A typical nineteenth-century slum in a jerry-built industrial town. These developments were put up to house the growing population of factory and mine workers who left the land to become wage labourers during the first half-century of the Industrial Revolution.

The big landowners who managed their estates wisely, and successful manufacturers, such as Matthew Boulton and Richard Arkwright, made fortunes and gave employment to a much larger professional class of men, including surveyors, engineers, doctors and lawyers. Later on in the nineteenth century their successors would employ their expertise to alleviate the appalling conditions in the hurriedly built and unhygienic towns.

Opposite: While Parliament acted in the early nineteenth century to control the working conditions of children in the cotton mills, the plight of young mine workers did not come under official scrutiny until 1842. This illustration is from that year: the semi-naked girl is the 'trapper' working a ventilation door, while two other children, the 'putters', heave a heavy load of coal.

CHAPTER THREE

Steaming Along

In the year that Wellington defeated Napoleon at Waterloo, an American tourist named Joseph Ballard crossed the Atlantic, keen to see how the victorious nation was faring. He wrote up his experiences as *England in 1815, being reflections and comments on a trip through Britain in the year of Waterloo*. What delighted him most was that he could travel on English roads at an impressive speed:

> I took passage on Saturday in the coach for Warrington eighteen miles distant from Liverpool. …I was much amused at the activity of the tumbling boys who turned head over heels at the side of the coach and with such swiftness as to even keep up with it for some time, which is done in expectation that the passengers will throw them a penny, their parents being so miserably poor that this is resorted to as a means of subsistence.

> There were six passengers inside, and twelve outside the coach, besides the coachman and an abundance of luggage. This, added to the weight of the vehicle (which is generally two tons or more), makes it almost incredible that they should be able to go at the rate of seven and eight miles per hour. There is not the least derogation from respectability in riding upon the outside. I should certainly myself give it the preference in fine weather as you are enabled to have a finer view of the country through which you pass than when inside the coach. The danger is however greater in the event of an accident happening to the coach, but as they are made so very strong they are in a degree guarded.

SPEED AND STYLE

Although the Prince Regent, the future George IV, and his entourage had been known to terrify the locals by whipping up the horses and reaching the dangerous speed of 14 mph on occasions, this was quite impossible on nearly every mile of road in the kingdom. Goods wagons were doing well between London and Bath if they averaged 2–3 mph. As Ballard remarked, 7–8 mph for a laden passenger coach was sensational. Between 1750 and the building of the first commercial railways in the 1830s everyone was aware of the fact that travel on Britain's roads had been speeding up, almost imperceptibly at first, and then dramatically from 1815. It all depended on which bit of road you were on, as observed by Louis Simon, a wealthy New York merchant, who visited England in 1810–11 and could afford to take the best and most expensive transport from Bath to London. In his *Journal of a Tour and Residence in Great Britain* (1815) he described the journey, which began on relatively poor minor roads out of the West Country spa town.

By 1825, when this well-sprung barouche carriage took to the English roads, they had been greatly improved by John McAdam.

The roads are far from magnificent; they are generally just wide enough for two carriages; without ditches, not deep. A high artificial bank of stone and earth, with bushes growing on the top, too often intercepts all view beyond the next bend of the road, not a hundred yards of which is visible at one time. The horses are in general weak and tired, and unmercifully whipt, – so much so, as to induce us often to interfere in their behalf, choosing rather to go slower than to witness such cruelty.

The going changes dramatically when the coach reaches one of the newly re-surfaced post roads to London:

The country is beautiful, rich and varied with villas and mansions, and dark groves of pines, – shrubs in full bloom, lawns ever green, and gravel walks so neat, – with porter's lodges, built in rough-cast, and stuck all over with flints in their native grotesqueness; for this part of England is a great bed of chalk, full of this singular production [flints]. They are broken to pieces with hammers, and spread over the road in thick layers, forming a hard and even surface, upon which the wheels of carriages make no impression. The roads are now wider; kept in good repair, and not deep, notwithstanding the season. The post-horses excellent; and post boys riding instead of sitting. Our rate of travelling does not exceed six miles an hour, stoppages included; but we might go faster if we desired it. We meet with very few post-chaises, but a great many stage-coaches, mails &c. and enormous broad-wheel wagons. The comfort of the inns is our incessant theme at night, – the pleasure of it not yet worn out.

To travel in the style described by Louis Simon was expensive, and way beyond the means of the average Englishman. Competition was forcing fares down and greatly improving time-keeping, but there were many other expenses a traveller had to pay, as Joseph Ballard discovered in 1815:

The stage fare from Manchester to Liverpool, distance forty miles, is only six shillings. This is caused by the strong opposition, as there are eight or ten coaches continually running between those places. Besides the fare in the coach you have to pay the coachman one shilling per stage of about thirty miles, and the same to the guard whose business it is to take care of the luggage, &c. &c. Should the passenger refuse to pay the accustomed tribute he would inevitably be insulted. …The stagecoaches are very convenient and easy. No baggage is permitted to be taken inside, it being stowed away in the boot places before and behind the carriage for that purpose. Here it rides perfectly safe, not being liable to be rubbed, as they ride upon the same springs that the passengers do. A person can always calculate upon being at the place he takes the coach for (barring accidents) at a certain time, as the coachman is allowed a given time to go his stage. The guard always has a chronometer with him (locked up so that he cannot move the hands) as a guide with regard to time.

A coachman with a chronometer! It was more likely a 'carriage clock', but to have any time-keeper at all was a far cry from the days when the road journey from London to Bath took several days and it was routine for a woman barber to shave the men passengers en route at Axminster. Something very extraordinary had clearly happened on Britain's roads, which, during the Regency period, carried a formidable array of carriages of ingenious design, some with spring suspension. The post-chaise, in which there was no coachman and the four horses were driven by boys who straddled them, was one of the nippiest models. These were hired, and the boys who drove them were known as 'tigers', from their yellow uniforms. Dr Johnson told his biographer James Boswell in 1777: 'If…I had no duties and no reference to futurity, I would spend my life driving briskly in a post-chaise with a pretty woman.'

In the heyday of the great road revival, the very wealthiest had their own carriages for long-distance travel, and on the toll roads (as on the motorways in Europe today) they, like everyone else, had to pay a fee at the turnpike gate. In 1829 the charge of the Bath Trust, which ran a section of the road to London, was four pence 'for every horse or beast drawing any coach, barouche, sociable, berlin, chariot, landau, chaise, phaeton, curricle, gig, caravan, cart upon springs, hearse, litter or other light carriage except stage coaches'. The turnpike trusts, which collected the tolls, were run by leading local landowners, politicians, clergymen and businessmen. In *Macadam: The McAdam Family and the Turnpike Roads 1798–1861*, William Reader writes:

The trustees represented the land-owing and farming interests in the countryside; the trading, professional and banking interests in the market towns. They usually met in one of the posting houses which relied on the coaching trade for their living… Many trusts let their tolls at auction, which provided a guaranteed level of income and relieved the trustees of direct supervision of the gatekeepers, who were employed by the toll-farmers.

An eighteenth-century view of the gatehouse at the busy Tottenham Court Road turnpike by Thomas Rowlandson. All traffic passing through the barrier had to pay a toll.

Some of these toll-farmers were very wealthy: one named Lewis Levy was said to have made a fortune of £500,000 on tolls collected on roads within 60 miles of London.

ROAD MAINTENANCE AND REPAIR

Clearly, by the 1820s there had been a revolution in road transport. But it had been a long time coming. For centuries the roads in Britain had been neglected. In the mid-eighteenth century most of the main routes were in a worse state than they had been when the Romans left Britain in AD 420. With the rapid growth of new industries and new towns, the increase in traffic caused a crisis. Neglected roads were torn to pieces by heavily laden wagons, which were easy prey to highwaymen as the cruelly whipped horses strained to haul them from deep ruts. There were potholes 4 feet deep in some places, and it was not a rare accident for a toppled coachman or passenger to drown in them in wet weather. And the packhorse trains were in continual conflict.

Thomas Mace, one of the clerks of Trinity College, Cambridge, gave an account of the state of the Great North Road in 1657. Much of the ground, he said, was in terrible condition:

> …now spoiled and trampled down in all wide roads, where coaches and
> carts take liberty to pick and chuse for their best advantages; besides, such
> sprawling and straggling of coaches and carts utterly confound the road in
> all wide places, so that it is not only unpleasurable, but extreme perplexin'
> and cumbersome both to themselves and all horse travellers. [There are]
> innumerable controversies, quarrellings, and disturbances…daily
> committed by uncivil, refractory, and rude Russian-like rake-shames, in
> contesting for the way, too often proved mortal, and certainly were of
> very bad consequences to many.

In other words, pre-Restoration 'road rage'.

Before roads were improved in the last years of the eighteenth century, many goods were carried by packhorses, which could travel over rough tracks. Here timber is being taken to the lead mines at Allendale in Cumbria.

Although this was the age of invention of all kinds of machinery, the state of the roads was given little attention: better transport was badly needed, but improving the King's highway did not, for a long time, get the attention of imaginative minds. Responsibility for maintaining and repairing roads was divided up between thousands of trusts and authorities, who had little incentive to spend local funds on through traffic. In the seventeenth century the bulk of goods was carried by trains of packhorses, which did not really need good roads. It was the coming of the wagons, with their huge, creaking wheels and heavy loads, that churned up surfaces composed of crudely scattered earth and stone. It was not that there was no innovative scheme on offer, or that there were no laws passed to enable improvements to go ahead: those responsible for the roads simply were not interested.

Samuel Smiles, Victorian advocate of self-help, provides an amusing history of roads in his *Life of Thomas Telford* (1867). Each county had its own horror stories:

It was almost as difficult for old persons to get to church in Sussex during winter as it was in the Lincoln Fens, where they were rowed thither in boats. Fuller saw an old lady being drawn to church in her own coach by the aid of six oxen. The Sussex roads were indeed so bad as to pass into a by-word. A contemporary writer says, that in travelling a slough of extraordinary miryness, it used to be called 'the Sussex bit of the road'; and he satirically alleged that the reason why the Sussex girls were so long-limbed was because of the tenacity of the mud in that county; the practice of pulling the foot out of it 'by the strength of the ancle' tending to stretch the muscle and lengthen the bone.

As Smiles also reports, roads around London were no better:

…when the poet [Abraham] Cowley retired to Chertsey, in 1665, he wrote to his friend Sprat to visit him, and, by way of encouragement, told him that he might sleep the first night at Hampton town; thus occupying two days in the performance of a journey of twenty-two miles in the immediate neighbourhood of the metropolis. As late as 1736, we find Lord Hervey, writing from Kensington, complaining that 'the road between this place and London is grown so infamously bad that we live here in the same solitude as we would do if cast on a rock in the middle of the ocean; and all the Londoners tell us that there is between them and us an impassable gulf of mud'.

Thomas Mace, who had witnessed the horrors of the Great North Road, proposed the very sensible solution to the road problem, in verse:

First let the wayes be regularly brought
To artificial form, and truly wrought;
So that we can suppose them firmly mended,
And in all parts the work well ended,
That not a stone's amiss; but all compleat,
All lying smooth, round, firm, and wondrous neat.

It was to be another century before a road-maker of any talent was given the funds to construct a road 'all compleat'. The reason for this, according to Samuel Smiles, was simply that the administration of roads by so-called turnpike trusts was inefficient. But there was another reason: for a long time England looked to its rivers rather than its roads for the transport of heavy goods.

INLAND WATERWAYS

The uniquely favourable pattern of coast and river had given much of Britain a tremendous advantage over its European rivals in the age before canals were cut and roads improved. Navigable rivers, with tides running inland – for 60 miles in the case of the Thames – were all linked by the sea. As T. S. Willan points out in *River Navigation in England 1600 to 1750* (1964): 'From the point of view of inland navigation, the sea became merely a river around England.' This waterway network had been established since Roman times, and its existence was almost certainly the reason that roads were neglected for a long time.

Rivers offered convenient alternative routes to markets. Newcastle-upon-Tyne, for example, could send its coal to London by sea or river, and could also use river routes to other destinations, such as Cambridge and Abingdon. Cheshire cheese was shipped either westwards on the river Dee down to Bristol, or eastwards on the Trent to London and other southern ports. Butter from the Yorkshire Dales could be loaded on the Ouse and sent not only to London, but to all the other river ports in the country. In the case of heavy goods, such as coal, the cost of shipping was infinitely smaller than paying for lumbering wagons to haul it over the deplorable roads. Lighter goods could and did go by packhorse, as well as by wagon, but the importance of the river system, neglected until recently in accounts of the early Industrial Revolution, was huge.

Like all transport routes, rivers had their problems. There were conflicts between those wanting to use rivers as highways, and those who harnessed their power to drive mills, or spanned it with weirs to catch fish. As the wheels of industrialism began to turn a little faster in the early eighteenth century, the competing demands on rivers became more problematic. The so-called 'water poet' John Taylor had anticipated the problems when he wrote of his experiences working on the Thames and rivers to the west in a poem called 'Taylor's Last Voyage':

> *I truely treate that men may note and see*
> *What blessings Navigable Rivers bee,*
> *And how that thousands are debarr'd those blessings*
> *By few mens avaritous hard oppressings*

Before there was any concerted effort to improve the roads, and when the notion of cutting an entirely new canal system was still an idle dream, a good deal of time and money was spent in attempting to improve the navigability of rivers. There were schemes to connect the Thames and the Severn, proposals to open up small rivers by widening and dredging, and for cutting canals to connect rivers and do away with the need for land links: in other words, for engineering to turn the natural advantages of the rivers linked by the sea into a truly national network of waterways.

To raise money for these schemes, 'pound locks' were created, very similar to those that still exist today on canals, and a toll was charged on all boats passing through. Taylor the water poet refers to the locks as turnpikes. In the late seventeenth century there were three between Oxford and the village of Bercot. An account of them, given in a contemporary history of Oxfordshire, describes how floodgates were put across the river: 'Within these there is a large square taken out of the river, built up each side with free-stone, big enough to receive the largest barge afloat; and at the other end another pair of flood-gates, opening and shutting, and having sluices like the former. Which is the whole fabrick of a turn-pike.'

As can be imagined, river turnpike tolls were no more popular then than road tax or parking fines are today, and the communities that were supposed to benefit from the toll income resented spending any money on maintaining locks, in just the same way as the turnpike trusts disliked improving the roads. And the big problem with river navigation was that it had to a large extent given rise to a distribution of towns and industries that was being radically altered by the rise of new mines and factories. Although some canals were cut, and some river improvements made, most schemes came to very little. At the same time, the neglect of the roads, now carrying more and more wagon traffic, created a transport crisis that had to be tackled in a new way.

CANALS LEAD THE WAY

In continental Europe canals had been cut for centuries. The most spectacular of these – the Canal du Midi – had been constructed in France (1667–94), linking Bordeaux and the Atlantic with Sète on the Mediterranean. It had been conceived and promoted by Pierre-Paul Riquet, who had made his fortune as a salt tax collector, and it was a project for his retirement. Work had begun in the same year as the Fire of London – 1666. It was a fantastic success, as well as a great feat of engineering, which involved the creation of a reservoir to maintain water levels in the canal during the summer. The value of it was obvious: ships no longer had to circumnavigate the treacherous Bay of Biscay and the southern coast of Portugal to reach the Mediterranean.

The Canal du Midi was one of the sights of the Grand Tour of Europe, popular with the aristocracy and the well-to-do in the eighteenth century. It was of special interest to a young man who had coal mines on his Lancashire estates – Francis Egerton, the 3rd and last Duke of Bridgewater. His father had died when he was young, his mother remarried and more or less ignored him, and his older brothers died of tuberculosis, leaving him sole heir to Worsley Estate and a coal fortune. He went to Eton, but spent his holidays at Tatton Hall in Cheshire, where he was cared for by his cousin, Samuel Egerton, who acted as his guardian. When he was twenty-one and a rather sickly young man he was sent off on the Grand Tour and saw the Canal du Midi at Lyons on the Rhône.

A map of the Canal du Midi, a feat of engineering that was to inspire the young Duke of Bridgewater, who later became a pioneer of canals in England.

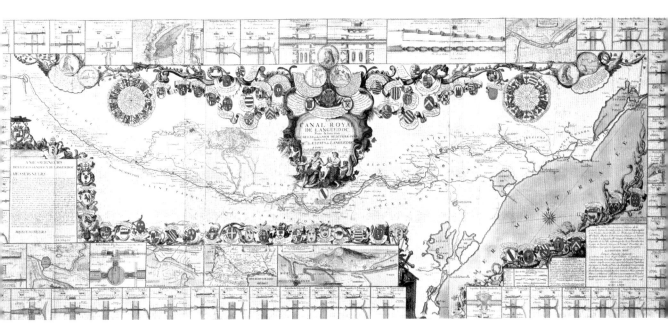

Returning to England, he fell in love with a widow, whom he wanted to marry. A scandal in her family put an end to their engagement, so he returned to Lancashire and his estate, where he became interested in a scheme his father had floated in 1737, the year after Francis was born, to cut a canal to make shipment of Worsley coal more efficient. It would have linked Worsley with the Mersey and Irwell Navigation, one of the improved rivers, but it had come to nothing. Inspired by the Canal du Midi and its impressive system of locks, Francis discussed reviving the scheme with his cousin at Tatton Hall, and with the Earl Gower, his brother-in-law, who had an agent called Thomas Gilbert. Francis took on Gilbert's younger brother, John, and they laid plans for a new canal to link Worsley with Salford. Permission to start work was granted in a Parliamentary Act of 1759.

When they looked around for someone who could build their canal, they were fortunate to find John Brindley, known both to the Earl Gower and the Duke's guardian. Brindley was then in his early forties and had gained a wide reputation as a competent and inventive engineer. He was born in 1716 in Leek, Derbyshire, and it seems that his father, a farmer, owned a small amount of land. Romanticising Brindley, Samuel Smiles described his father as a wastrel, and for many years it was believed that Brindley was illiterate. In fact, he could read and write, and fathom at least basic mathematics. At the age of seventeen he was apprenticed to a millwright, and was from then on involved in a great many schemes, which became grander as his reputation spread. He put up a windmill for the Wedgwoods in the Potteries, and devised all kinds of pumping machines, using steam as well as water power. In 1758 the Earl Gower and other promoters asked Brindley to survey the land for a prospective canal to link Liverpool and the Mersey with the Potteries.

Brindley went to work and drew up plans for the 93-mile canal, which would become his greatest achievement, involving five tunnels, 213 bridges, 160 aqueducts and seventy-six locks. But the start of building was delayed for eight years. Meanwhile, by 1759 John Gilbert had heard of Brindley's great scheme, which involved the idea of a Grand Trunk Canal as a central artery, and suggested that he would be the man for the Duke of Bridgewater's project. When Brindley looked at the existing plans he declared that he could better them, creating a canal that would link Worsley with the proposed Grand Trunk Canal, and therefore not only with Manchester, but all the other major centres: Liverpool, Birmingham and London. With a nod of approval from the Duke, he spent forty-six days at Worsley, surveying the land and drawing up his scheme.

What Brindley had in mind was revolutionary. All canals cut up to that time had been lateral, that is to say, they joined rivers and followed the contours of

existing valleys. The Duke of Bridgewater's Worsley canal would be arterial – an entirely new waterway that would travel over the existing landscape, tunnel under hills, run through cuttings with embankments, and cross rivers. It was a prototype for the building of railways, as they too could not cope with steep gradients. All Brindley's experience and ingenuity went into the many works involved, and the innovation that impressed the visitors who flocked to see the first sections of the completed canal was the Barton Aqueduct, which carried barges, as one excited observer said, 'as high as the tree-tops'. Although the Romans had built aqueducts all over Europe (the Pont du Gard, which took mountain water to the town of Nîmes in southern France is one of the most famous), nobody before had seen the

The Barton Aqueduct, built by John Brindley to carry barges on the Duke of Bridgewater's canal near Manchester, was a wonder of the age.

89

likes of Brindley's 'airborne' canal in Britain. In fact, some doubted that it would hold water, despite the engineer's assurance that a lining of clay would do the job.

While canals were impressive in engineering terms, the legislation that governed their use was quite the opposite. Like the present-day rules for operating British railways, the owner of the system could not run the transport that travelled on it. This made the economics difficult for those like the Duke of Bridgewater who had invested so much in their construction. The Worsley canal lowered the price of coal, but brought no instant profits. Brindley, however, went on to build a staggering number of canals, as they became the fashionable solution to the country's transport problem.

One of Brindley's greatest projects was the cutting of the canal that connected the rivers Trent and Mersey: Brindley liked to call it the Grand Trunk because it was intended to become part of a network of canals. Work began in 1766 on a 92-mile route that would take the canal through three tunnels. The longest of these, burrowing under Harecastle Hill, was more than a mile and a half long. It was cut by miners working mostly by candlelight, and was plagued with problems. Brindley literally worked himself to death, dying in 1772, five years before the Harecastle Tunnel was completed and the full length of the canal opened.

It was an astonishing achievement for its time. The excavations began at both ends, and accurate surveying of the ground ensured that they met in the middle. But the Harecastle Tunnel soon proved to be a bottleneck on the Trent and Mersey Canal. There were no towpaths and the canal boats, which were normally drawn by horses, had no motor, so had to be 'legged' through by men pushing against the brick walls with their feet. Brindley's tunnel was replaced later by a much wider tunnel, with two paths engineered by Thomas Telford.

ROAD-MAKING REVIVED

As 'canal mania' took off, and the dream of linking all towns and industrial centres with waterways was realised, the first of a new breed of road engineer appeared and began to transform the muddy tracts in his native Yorkshire, as well as to cut new routes across boggy moorland. A tall, striking figure, who walked with a wooden staff, he had been blind since childhood, which made his achievements even more remarkable. He was born John Metcalf in Knaresborough, Yorkshire, in 1718, and, like so many children at the time, was left blind at the age of six after suffering from smallpox, the hideous disease that took so many lives during the eighteenth century. Nicknamed 'Blind Jack', he became a celebrated local character around whom legends gathered. Despite his lack of sight, he was said to be able to find his way anywhere, ride a horse, rescue the drowning and perform incredible feats

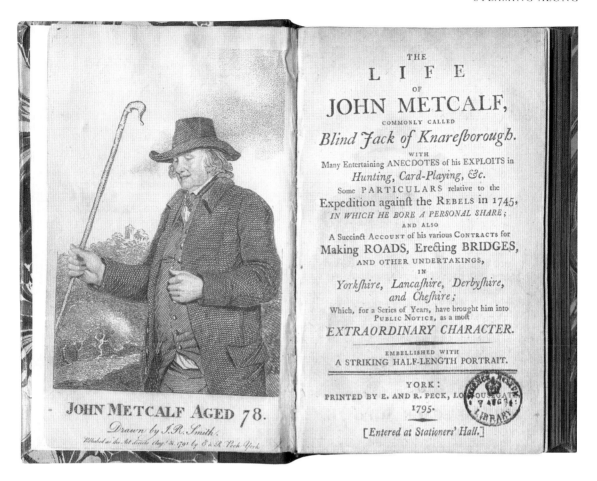

JOHN METCALF AGED 78.

Drawn by I.R.Smith.

Publised as the Act directs Aug.t 31, 1795 by E & R. Peck York.

THE
LIFE
OF
JOHN METCALF,
COMMONLY CALLED
Blind Jack of Knaresborough.
WITH
Many Entertaining ANECDOTES of his EXPLOITS in
Hunting, Card-Playing, &c.
Some PARTICULARS relative to the
Expedition against the REBELS in 1745,
IN WHICH HE BORE A PERSONAL SHARE;
AND ALSO
A Succinct ACCOUNT of his various CONTRACTS for
Making ROADS, Erecting BRIDGES,
AND OTHER UNDERTAKINGS,
IN
Yorkshire, Lancashire, Derbyshire,
and Cheshire;
Which, for a Series of Years, have brought him into
PUBLIC NOTICE, as a most
EXTRAORDINARY CHARACTER.

EMBELLISHED WITH
A STRIKING HALF-LENGTH PORTRAIT.

YORK:
PRINTED BY E. AND R. PECK, LOW-OUSEGATE.
1795.
[Entered at Stationers' Hall.]

in almost every sphere. How much of Blind Jack's biography is fiction is impossible to say, but it is certain he was an accomplished violinist and that he travelled widely about the country, on one occasion in his youth to escape his responsibilities as the father of an illegitimate child.

He is said to have fought with the Duke of Cumberland at the Battle of Culloden in 1746, and to have played his violin to the victorious troops afterwards. Summing up Metcalf's career to his mid-forties, Samuel Smiles, who singled him out for special commendation, wrote:

> His travels about the country as a guide to those who could see, as a musician, soldier, chapman, fish-dealer, horse-dealer, and waggoner, had given him a perfectly familiar acquaintance with the northern roads. He could measure timber or hay in the stack, and rapidly reduce their contents to feet and inches after a mental process of his own. Withal he

Although he lost his sight at the age of six, John Metcalf defied his disability and lived an adventurous life as a musician, soldier and engineer. Known as 'Blind Jack of Knaresborough', he became famous for his road-building in Yorkshire and other northern counties.

was endowed with an extraordinary activity and spirit of enterprise, which, had his sight been spared him, would probably have rendered him one of the most extraordinary men of his age. As it was, Metcalf now became one of the greatest of its road-makers and bridge-builders.

Metcalf had been operating a business carrying goods between Knaresborough and York when, in 1765, an Act was passed to allow the building of a turnpike between the Yorkshire spa town of Harrogate and Boroughbridge. The contract was let out in sections, and Blind Jack persuaded the surveyor in charge to give him the job of building the 3-mile section between Minskip and Fearnsby (now Fearby). He sold his carrier business and set to work, exploiting a local quarry for stone to be broken for the road surface. In fact, he produced such a fine surface that he was soon commissioned to build more sections of the turnpike. What he lacked in knowledge of engineering he made up for in boldness, running roads over boggy ground by creating foundations with packed furze from the heaths. As his reputation spread, he worked in Lancashire and other counties. He even built bridges, calculating in his head what the dimensions should be and dictating them to others, who drew up the plans, which he could not see himself.

At that time the length of roads was measured with a device called a viameter, which was a wooden wheel of a specific circumference pushed along on a frame with a handle, each revolution registering on a readable dial. Blind Jack had one adapted for his own use, with a meter that he could check by touch. A replica of this device is wheeled out for celebrations of the life of this local hero at present-day Knaresborough festivals.

Smiles estimated that Metcalf, by the end of his road-building career – he lived until he was ninety-three – had built 180 miles of turnpike road, all of which were regarded as superior to anything in existence. On one occasion he sensed the ground beneath him altered and asked the men to dig down. They found an old Roman road, and promptly smashed up the stone and incorporated it into the new highway – good for traffic, but disappointing for archaeology.

However, Blind Jack on his own, despite his apparently super-human powers, could do no more than chip away at the national problem of road transport, and there appears to have been nobody else at the time who followed his example. Although the number of turnpike trusts was growing, they continued to be lackadaisical in their approach to road-making. This was a shame, because the eighteenth-century engineers were turning their attention to the possibility of carriages that had no need of a horse and might run on broader, and less destructive, wheels.

HORSELESS CARRIAGES

The idea of a steam-driven carriage had been around for a very long time. Sir Isaac Newton had prophesied that one day people would travel at 50 mph, and in his *Explanations of the Newtonian Philosophy* (1680) he included a charming drawing of a vehicle propelled forwards by a jet of steam: it was a kind of boiler on wheels. The Frenchman Denys Papin made a little model steam carriage in the 1690s, and there were accounts of steam vehicles in China. However, the idea was not taken too seriously until the invention of the first atmospheric pumping engines. Thomas Savery talked of using steam for a horseless carriage at the end of the seventeenth century, and the idea was becoming less fanciful by the 1750s. The doctor Erasmus Darwin discussed the possibility with both Matthew Boulton and James Watt, and wrote in 1761: 'As I was riding home yesterday, I considered the scheme of the fiery chariot, and the longer I contemplated this favourite idea, the more practical it appeared to me.'

Just eight years later, legend has it that the very first working steam vehicle, designed as a gun-carriage, had had a trial run in the grounds of the Arsenal in Paris. It was the invention of a military engineer from the Lorraine region, Nicholas Joseph Cugnot, who had retired from the army at the age of forty, and was given public funds for his experiments. Cugnot's steam wagon was a three-wheeler, with pistons powering the single front wheel, and moved hesitantly at about 2½ mph. It could carry fuel for only fifteen or twenty minutes, but it was said to have worked when first put to the test in 1769 with four passengers.

According to French legend, this wonderful wagon, designed by Nicholas Cugnot in 1769, was the first working steam carriage in history. Recent studies of the original suggest that with a full boiler it would have fallen on its nose.

Encouraged by his first success, Cugnot made some modifications, and in 1770 took his new model out on to the Paris streets. He was running at 3 mph when he took a corner too sharply and the machine overbalanced. The Cugnot carriage was banned, and he was put in jail. He was then pardoned and given a small pension, losing it during the French Revolution, and regaining it under Napoleon, until his death in 1804 at the age of seventy-five. Cugnot's engine is now in the Musée des Arts et Métiers in Paris. (It is a wonderful-looking juggernaut, but recent studies suggest that it would never have worked and that the Cugnot story, popular with French schoolchildren, is a fable.)

Dr Erasmus Darwin and other steam-carriage visionaries were forever bothering James Watt with the idea, but he would become irritated with it and instead got on with his designs for stationary engines. However, in 1777 the Soho works in Birmingham took on an eccentric young Scotsman called William Murdoch (sometimes spelt 'Murdock'), who had worked as a millwright and impressed Matthew Boulton with his unusual hat. When Boulton asked what it was made of, Murdoch said in his Scots brogue: 'Timmer, sir.' It was made of wood, and though it was oval in shape, it had been turned by Murdoch on a lathe. That got him a job at the Soho works – he had walked from Scotland to Birmingham – and later, during his spare time when he was based in Cornwall, he devised a working model of a steam locomotive that ran in circles around the living room of his home. His first model was completed in 1784, and was still in working order a century later.

A new and exciting age of the steam carriage did not appear to be far off. Another Scottish engineer, William Symington, had a model steam coach working in 1786, and adapted his engine to propel boats. He was more successful on water than on land, and had a working pleasure boat in 1788. In 1801 a Symington steamboat was operating on the Forth and Clyde Canal. It was

A cartoonist's vision of steam wagons on the Whitechapel Road, London, in 1830. There was a time before the advent of 'railway mania' when many believed this would be the future, with steam vehicles racing along the new macadam roads.

named the *Charlotte Dundas* by Symington's patron, Lord Dundas, and made use of James Watt's innovation, the 'separate condenser'. The Duke of Bridgewater ordered eight of these boats for his canals, but died before the order was fulfilled.

In the same year that Symington's steamboat plied the Forth and Clyde Canal, a Cornish engineer named Richard Trevithick succeeded in making the first working steam-driven road vehicle in Britain. Born in 1771 to a mining family, Trevithick first turned his hand to making high-pressure pumping engines, a design he arrived at to get around the existing patents held by Watt and Boulton. Although he had little formal education and was described by his schoolmaster as slow and obstinate, Trevithick had a genius for mechanics. He was a big man, 6 feet 2 inches tall, a wrestler nicknamed the 'Cornish Giant'.

From 1796, Trevithick made model steam locomotives, which he showed friends at his home in Camborne. By Christmas Eve 1801 he had completed his first full-scale model four-wheeler, with a copper boiler and a funnel very like an early steam train. There was great local interest in Trevithick's machine, which was put together in a variety of workshops, and when locals heard him firing it up for the first time on the road, there was a scramble to get on board. In his *Steam on Common Roads* (1891) William Fletcher gives a first-hand account from one of the Camborne men who took a ride that Christmas Eve:

This is not a toy train set, but a full-scale working model with which the Cornish inventor Richard Trevithick entertained Londoners in Euston Square in 1808. His steam locomotive, called Catch Me Who Can, *could travel at 12 miles an hour, but it was too heavy for existing rail technology, and ran for only two months.*

When we saw Trevithick was going to turn on steam, we jumped on as many as could, maybe seven or eight of us. 'Twas a stiffish hill going up to Camborne Beacon, but she went off like a little bird. When she had gone about a quarter of a mile, there was a rough piece of road, covered with loose stones. She didn't go quite so fast, and as it was a flood of rain, and we were very much squeezed together, I jumped off. She was going faster than I could walk, and went up the hill about half a mile further when they turned her, and came back again to the shop.

On Christmas Day, Trevithick went visiting in his new-fangled machine. Within a week or so, he was making journeys of 3 miles and more, though there were a few accidents when the locomotive turned over. It came to an unfortunate end when it caught fire and burnt out while Trevithick was in a pub. The vehicle had been made in the workshop of Captain Andrew Vivian, and he went into partnership with Trevithick. A new, improved model was made, and at the end of 1801 they took this machine up to London to apply for a patent, which they were awarded in March 1802. While in London, they rode around the streets, going one day from the carriage shop in Leather Lane, down Grays Inn Road, past Lord's cricket ground, to Paddington and back by way of Islington. Vivian did the steering and Trevithick the stoking, and in this way they rattled through Tottenham Court Road to Euston at 8–10 mph. There were demonstrations of the Trevithick engine in Oxford Street, with the road cleared of horse traffic for safety. And then the inevitable crash, when they ran into a wall.

In 1804 Trevithick designed a steam engine to run on rails, which had a trial in a Welsh colliery that had carriages drawn by horses on metal rails. It worked, but the crudely made cast-iron rails were not strong enough to take the weight of the steam engine, and there the experiment rested. In 1808 Trevithick ran a steam locomotive on a small circle of track in an arena at Euston, London, offering the public rides at a shilling a time. But his main business remained the building and selling of steam engines for mines, and he sold some to Peru in South America. When problems arose with these in 1816, he sailed there to sort them out. He did not return to England and his wife and family for ten years. In Peru he quarrelled with the owners of the silver mine who had bought his engines, and to recoup his losses took on work as an adviser and opened his own mine. He got involved in the war there with the Spanish, designed a gun, and then escaped home, having lost everything. Poor Trevithick would have been buried in a pauper's grave in 1833 had his workmates not raised the money for a proper funeral. There are now Trevithick societies all over the world dedicated to his memory and achievements.

MACADAM ROADS

Experiments with steam carriages continued after Trevithick's death, and by the 1830s there were regular services running. These, along with the horse-drawn stages, coaches and wagons, were able to take advantage of the spectacular road improvements that had begun around 1816 under the supervision of a Scotsman who was to lend his name to highways not only in Britain, but all over the world: John Loudon McAdam. Of all the bizarre stories of innovation and individual initiative in the dynamic half century of the first Industrial Revolution, there is none to match that of this extraordinary character. By the 1820s the term 'macadam' was in the language and meant a good road surface, hard and dry,

A lampoon of John Loudon McAdam, who, at the age of sixty, became a celebrated road-builder, lending his name to a new kind of surface composed of broken stone pieces no bigger than walnuts. Tarmacadam came later.

which allowed horse-drawn coaches to travel at maximum speeds in both winter and summer. Nearly 1500 years after the Romans had left, Britain had a decent road system again.

John McAdam had absolutely no engineering knowledge, and did not start work in earnest on his project until he was sixty years old. He was born in 1756, the youngest of ten children of James McAdam, a minor laird, and Susannah Cochrane, a niece of the 7th Earl of Dundonald. The family were not rich, but they were, by the standards of the day, not badly off. When James died in 1770 he left John an estimated £1000, a fair sum for a fourteen-year-old boy. With this small fortune, John went to New York, then still a British colony, to be cared for by an uncle, William McAdam, who was a merchant and had been involved in founding the New York Chamber of Commerce. For a while, John worked for his uncle, and then set up in business himself as a prize-master, dealing in goods seized from enemy ships. He appears to have had only a minor role in the War of Independence in 1776, serving as a loyalist against the rebels. Two years later he married a Miss Glorianna Margaretta Nicoll of Suffolk County, Long Island, whom a contemporary account described as 'a young lady of great beauty and merit with a large fortune'. Her father was a prominent lawyer, who was in charge of the New York Assembly when it declared itself independent of Britain. Although he wanted to stay on after the Revolution, John McAdam had picked the wrong side, so found himself, with his wife and children, back in Scotland in 1783.

McAdam had done well and was able to buy himself a substantial estate in Ayrshire, where he lived in style. A man in his position was expected to take public office, and in 1787 he became one of the trustees of the Ayrshire turnpike roads, and later a deputy lieutenant. He went into business with a relative, founding the British Tar Company, which had a patent system for extracting tar from coal. The tar was intended for ships, not for turnpike roads, as the idea of using tar to produce a smooth surface had not yet been thought of. For reasons that are obscure, this tar company got into trouble, and McAdam ended up in debt. He sold his Ayrshire estate and moved to Falmouth in Cornwall. Exactly what he was up to, nobody is sure, but one unpublished biography suggests that he was back in business as a prize-master, handling goods seized from French vessels who were at war with the British. This came to an end when peace was restored in 1802, and McAdam was on the move again, this time to Bristol.

At this stage of his life, McAdam obviously had money, but nobody has been able to discover where it was coming from. From 1798 he travelled a great deal between his problematic tar company in Scotland and the south of England, gaining an intimate knowledge of the state of the roads in the process. His service with the Ayrshire turnpike trusts had given him an interest in the subject of road-building, and, according to his own account given in evidence in 1819 to a House of Commons Select Committee on highways, he made his inspection of roads a 'sort of business'. He estimated that between 1798 and 1814 he had travelled 30,000 miles. In doing so, he set himself up as a kind of independent investigator, calling on turnpike trusts all over the country, and quizzing them about their finances and methods of operation. He took a dim view of them, and reckoned that about an eighth of the money raised for road-building was wasted.

Although he had no knowledge of the practicalities of road-building when he set out, he questioned surveyors and those who worked on the roads. He was generally greeted with suspicion and had a hard time of it, and in 1811 became unwell. Just when he was about to abandon his project, he was asked by Sir John Sinclair, president of the Board of Agriculture, to give evidence to the House of Commons on the state of the roads. His report, 'Observations on the Highways of the Kingdom', was appended to a Select Committee report, which he published himself as 'Remarks on the Present System of Road Making'.

McAdam made the point emphatically that everyone was approaching the problem of roads in the wrong way. They were trying to devise vehicles that could survive badly made highways when they should have been building better roads. He had spent twenty-six years travelling the country and had compared methods of construction. There were only a few roads that he regarded as well made: one in Somerset, one in Westmorland (perhaps a Blind Jack Metcalf creation, though he is never mentioned) and one near Bristol. In each case, the surface was composed of small stones 'no bigger than a walnut', spread about 6 inches thick so that the action of traffic bedded them down. The only bit of 'science' McAdam had devised was that the point of contact between a wagon wheel and the road was just 1 inch, and that 'every piece of stone put into a road which exceeds an inch in any of its dimensions is mischievous'.

All that was required for road improvement all over the country, he declared, was for the turnpike trustees to excavate the lumps of stone and earth that had been laid down haphazardly, break them into small bits, and lay them down again in the manner he prescribed so that highways were exactly what their name suggested – higher than the surrounding land. They did not need to bring in new raw materials: it was all there. He gave an account of his 'Directions for Repairing a Road' to the House of Commons Select Committee on Highways and Turnpike Roads in 1810.

> The stone in the road is to be loosened up to the depth of a foot, and broken so as to pass through a screen or harp of an inch in the opening, by which no stone above an inch in any of its dimensions can be admitted.

> The road is then to be laid as flat as possible, if it is not hollow in the middle it is sufficient; the less it is rounded the better; water cannot stand upon a level surface. The broken stone is then to be laid evenly on it, but if half or six inches is laid first, and exposed a short time to the pressure of carriages, and then a second coat of six inches laid on, it has been found advantageous in consolidating the materials.

McAdam wanted to prove his point with some experiments, but nobody took him up on the offer. Instead, in 1816, at the age of sixty, he accepted the post of general surveyor of the Bristol roads.

To begin with, his job was like that of a modern managerial troubleshooter. There was fierce resistance to his plans from the corrupt and mostly bankrupt turnpike trusts, which for years had been run by local bigwigs who wanted responsibility for no stretch of road longer than they could ride to trust meetings and back home in a day. Surveyors resented McAdam's intrusion, and bit by bit he replaced them with family members. Very soon he was able to show that he could produce better roads more cheaply than before. About a third of road-building costs went in wages to the workmen, who broke up the stones and re-laid them. In the past 'statue labour' – a kind of community service workforce – had been widely used, but this was not exactly enthusiastic about road work. Some of the new workforce was cheap farm labour, which came from the agricultural depression that had occurred at the end of the Napoleonic Wars in 1815.

Many of McAdam's innovations were nothing to do with construction, which was extremely simple. His strategy was to get rid of incompetent surveyors and pay labourers only for what they achieved – piece work as opposed to a daily rate. Although his methods caused resentment locally, his fame soon spread, and he was consulted by turnpike trusts around the country, apparently offering his advice free of charge. It is estimated that he and numerous members of the McAdam clan whom he appointed as surveyors were responsible for more than 3000 miles of road in England and Wales, and 400 miles in Scotland. In 1826 his son James was made surveyor for the roads north of London, and the family fame spread to America.

McAdam was not without rivals or critics. The Scottish stonemason turned engineer Thomas Telford, who was just a year younger than McAdam, turned his attention to road-making and in 1814 was given a budget of £50,000 – a huge sum for the Treasury to put up – to remake the road between Carlisle and Glasgow, a project regarded as of national importance. While Telford was in agreement with McAdam about the appalling administration of roads, he strongly disagreed with his methods of construction. He insisted on laying down a solid hardcore beneath the surface of small stones, and argued that McAdam's roads would not last. The two great road-builders fought it out before a Select Committee in the House of Commons in 1819, Telford having engineering expertise on his side, while McAdam insisted that his roads were much cheaper to construct. Between them, with their different methods, they completely transformed the road system in Britain, only to see it fall into decline with the coming of the railways.

This was already happening in 1836 when John McAdam, in his eightieth year, died in Moffat, Ayrshire. He lived in Bristol, but in his seventies took to the road again, travelling in a two-horse carriage that was followed by an untethered pony and a Newfoundland dog that made sure the pony did not wander off. When he wanted to visit somewhere en route or go shooting, he left the carriage and mounted the pony. He was about to return to Bristol when he died peacefully. He had already been involved, in a small way, as one of the promoters of a railway line between London and Bristol, although he had earlier been an enthusiastic advocate of steam-driven road vehicles which, with their weight and broad wheels, would have improved the macadam surface.

Overleaf: The Menai Straits road bridge, completed in 1826, was designed by the great engineer Thomas Telford.

101

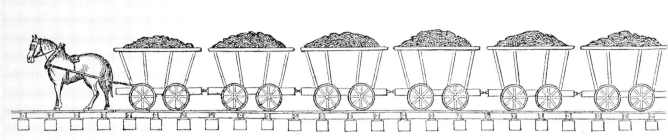

Long before steam
railways came into
being, wagons running
on wooden rails had
been used in mining
areas. Later horses
drew wagons on iron
rails that were not
strong enough to
carry steam engines.

RAIL TRAVEL

Although railways came to symbolise the triumph of the Industrial Revolution, and to overshadow all the innovations in transport that had gone before, the technique of running carriages on tracks went back to Elizabethan England. There are references to 'railes' used in coal mines from the late sixteenth century, and by the eighteenth century what were known as 'waggon ways' were common. The rails were wooden, with grooves cut to hold the wheels of wagons that were hauled by horse or pony. As these wagons could not be run on a steep incline, viaducts were built across rivers and streams, just as they were for Brindley's canals. Sometimes there was a slight gradient so that wagons could free-wheel in one direction, then be hauled back by horses.

George Stephenson, born in 1781, was brought up with steam and colliery rails. His father looked after the stationary engines at Deweley Colliery in Northumberland, and that is where he started work. In 1803, when his son Robert was an infant, George had met Richard Trevithick and was familiar with his steam vehicles. He was also familiar with the first successful steam engine to run on rails, which had been built by William Hedley, another engineer, working at Wylam Colliery. Trevithick had built the first 'Wylam locomotive', which ran on wooden rails, but this was not a success. In 1808 the first iron rails were brought in and Hedley was asked to design an engine that would run on them. There was a technical problem: engines designed like those that ran on roads, with independent wheels, slipped on the smooth rails. Working with a blacksmith, Hedley solved the problem by linking the wheels with cogs and letting the weight of the engine provide grip. The first successful train, the *Puffing Billy*, ran in 1813, and continued to work for many years.

THE "PUFFING BILLY" LOCOMOTIVE.

SCALE 1½ INCH = 1 FOOT.

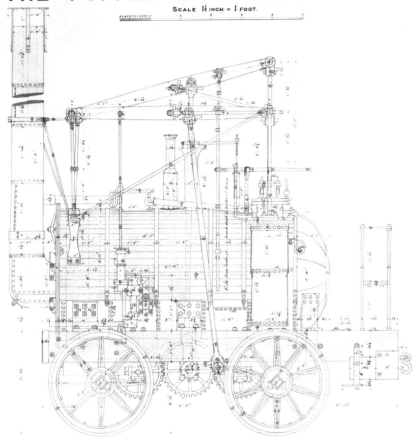

Side Elevation.

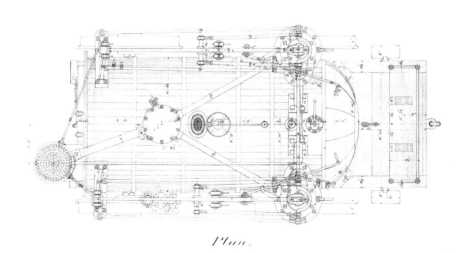

Plan.

*One of the first
working steam engines
running on rails,
William Hedley's
Puffing Billy hauled
coal wagons over a
5-mile track from
Wylam Colliery to
Lemington-on-Tyne,
Northumberland, from
1813 until 1861.
It is now preserved in
the Science Museum
in London.*

In 1814, George Stephenson improved on the 'Puffing Billy' with his engine the 'Blucher'. It ran on wooden rails at first, with the wheels coupled in pairs by a chain. In all, Stephenson made sixteen prototype steam trains, improving the design each time. When, in 1821, an Act allowed the building of a railway line between Stockton and Darlington, he was ready to make a bid. The original plan was for the wagons to be horse-drawn, but when Stephenson demonstrated his train, he was given the job of engineer. It was another four years before the triumphant opening of the Stockton–Darlington line in 1825. Cast-iron rails were now being produced, and Stephenson had greatly increased the power of his engine with the new model, the 'Locomotion'. The railway age had begun.

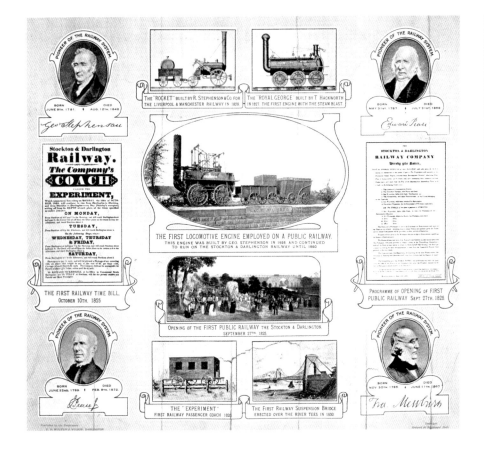

At first planned for horse-drawn carriages, the Stockton to Darlington Railway opened in 1825 with Stephenson's Locomotion *engine pulling carriages of paying passengers. This poster advertising the service marked the beginning of a new era in transport.*

Opposite: Canal builders, carving out level watercourses across rolling countryside by means of tunnels, bridges and cuttings, paved the way for railways, which, like canals, could not cope with steep gradients. This picture shows the Olive Mount cutting between Liverpool and Manchester in 1831.

CHAPTER FOUR

The Lure of London

On Friday 19 November 1762 the twenty-two-year-old James Boswell came in sight of London after a four-day journey from his family's estate in Scotland. He was in a post-chaise with one other passenger, a Mr Stewart, who was to ship on an East Indiaman from the London docks. Boswell was on his way to the greatest and most dazzling city in Europe, and could hardly contain his excitement: 'When we came upon Highgate Hill and had a view of London, I was all life and joy… I sung all manner of songs, and began to make one about an amorous meeting with a pretty girl, the burthen of which was as follows: "She gave me this, I gave her that, And tell me, had she not tit for tat?"'

The diaries Boswell kept during his stay in London in 1762 give a very intimate account of the fun he had in the capital, which was then a wonderfully entertaining place if you had money and connections. Boswell had both. He took pleasant lodgings in Pall Mall, and spent his time in coffee-houses, where he read the *Spectator* and other newspapers, in taverns and wandering the ill-lit streets. Notoriously, with his trusty 'armour', as he called his contraceptive sheath, used as a protection against venereal disease, he 'performed manfully' on Westminster Bridge with a prostitute he picked up in the streets. In Pall Mall he was close to St James's Park, where the Foot Guards drilled and members of the royal court strolled in daylight. After dark the park gates were locked, but about 6500 people had a key to it. In the early spring of 1763 Boswell records in his diary:

> As I was coming home this night, I felt carnal inclinations raging through my frame. I determined to gratify them. I went to St James's Park and…picked up a whore. For the first time did I engage in armour, which I found but dull satisfaction. She who submitted to my lusty embraces was a young Shropshire girl, only seventeen, very well-looked, her name Elizabeth Parker. Poor being, she has a sad time of it.

Opposite: Eighteenth-century Covent Garden was a hive of activity, the crowds and bustle reflecting the energy and excitement of a city undergoing rapid growth and change. Little wonder that visitors such as James Boswell were enraptured by its vigour.

LONDON EXPANDS

The London Boswell enjoyed had not yet been transformed by the many forces unleashed by industrialism, which were to make it barely recognisable fifty years later. Watermen on the Thames still provided the chief form of transport: there were stairs all the way along the riverbanks, where liveried wherrymen cried, 'Oars! Oars!' in search of custom. Although there were horse-drawn hackney carriages, there were no horse omnibuses other than the 'short' stagecoaches running in and out of London, and the sedan chair – an enclosed box carried on shafts by two men, one before and one behind – had not disappeared. In 1791 Horace Walpole thought that London had grown so big that 'Hercules and Atlas could not carry anybody from one end of the enormous capital to the other'. Several times he thought he saw from his coach a rioting mob, only to discover it was 'nymphs and swains sauntering or trudging'.

The great growth of London between 1750 and the first decades of the nineteenth century was fuelled by the new wealth created by the Industrial Revolution: it was the great marketplace, the centre of fashion, and where the landed aristocracy spent much of their riches. On the Thames, the congestion of shipping crammed into the Pool of London below London Bridge led to the building of a vast area of enclosed dockland from 1802 onwards. And though it was not, for the most part, in the forefront of technological change, London was a hive of industry, much of it geared to supplying the needs of the wealthy. The capital, which was sometimes described as a modern Babylon or Rome, was like a huge economic magnet.

To the east of the City of London, way beyond the built-up area on the Isle of Dogs, the West India Merchants Company established the first of the new docks, which were completed in 1802–3. The warehouses that lined the quays of the excavated dock basins stretched two-thirds of a mile, fine examples of the stark elegance of much Georgian commercial building. The one surviving warehouse, over which Canary Wharf now towers, has become the Museum in Docklands, with much of its original structure preserved. On 31 January 1805 the new London docks were opened, and soon afterwards the East India Company opened new docks at Blackwall, where it had had ship-building yards for a long time. Consequently, another huge region of the Isle of Dogs was excavated for the mooring of ships.

The final annihilation of the old port came with the carving out of St Katharine's Dock right on the eastern edge of the city. It took its name from the 700-year-old St Katharine's Hospital, which was demolished in the development, along with the homes of 11,300 riverside Londoners, most of whom were poor

Behind the elegant façades of early nineteenth-century London were terrible slums. This is George Cruickshank's illustration of Monmouth Street in Covent Garden, which accompanied Charles Dickens's Sketches by Boz, *published in 1836.*

and were offered no compensation. They had to make do, moving into mean streets with names such as Dark Entry, Cat's Hole, Shovell Alley and Pillory Lane.

Dockland attracted visitors in its early years, but it quickly became a world apart – a new East End that contrasted sharply with the new West End that had arisen from the mid-eighteenth century, and was still spreading over fields and marshland in the early 1800s. Some of the earth excavated for the new docks was taken up the Thames on barges and used as landfill for new estates, such as those of Belgravia.

111

A comfortable, middle-class home in leafy Hampstead during the 1820s. Providing furniture and clothing for the well-to-do was highly profitable for Matthew Boulton, Josiah Wedgwood and Richard Arkwright.

THE WEST END

The rise of London's West End had begun after the Great Fire of 1666, when the demand for new housing away from the charred ruins of the old town, with its tallow works and noxious industries, was satisfied by the development of new squares. This pattern continued and, with the growth in international trade, the concentration of wealth in London and then the huge increase in riches brought by the rise of industrialism, the West End extended far into the fields that marked its boundaries in Boswell's time.

An elite society composed of the families of the landed gentry and their various employees and hangers-on occupied the new developments, usually as leaseholders rather than owners. The Dukes of Westminster had a huge swathe of land known as the Grosvenor Estate, which included much of Mayfair, Grosvenor Square (first developed in the 1720s) and Belgravia (built from the 1820s). The town houses were only fully occupied during the London social season, when there was a great gathering in town, focusing around Parliament and the royal court. This usually began in the autumn and ended in spring or early summer.

A survey of the Grosvenor Mayfair estate in 1790 gave a detailed account of who lived and worked there, leaving out only the slum that had grown up just to the south of Oxford Street. Grosvenor Square itself had forty-seven households, of which thirty-one were occupied by titled aristocrats. The estate as a whole had thirty-seven peers, eighteen baronets, fifteen honourables and thirty-nine ladies. These made up about a tenth of all the inhabitants. In addition, there were government officials, such as Timothy Caswell, commissioner of the Salt Tax, the King's organist, army officers, doctors, architects and lawyers. But the largest group of inhabitants comprised tradesmen who lived over the shop: dairymen, masons, plumbers, cabinet-makers, tailors, dressmakers and fifty-five butchers, whose meat was driven into town on the hoof to be slaughtered on the premises. In 1801 a lady protested that she could not get out of her home in Brook Street, Mayfair, for 'fear of being gored by bullocks'. In the 1770s there were sheep in Cavendish Square, the 'poor things starting at every coach', as one disgruntled observer wrote.

For the aristocracy, who enjoyed rolling acres on their country estates, town life – however splendid their houses might seem to us today – was regarded as cramped. Foreign visitors were surprised there were so few town 'palaces' like those in Europe, and thought twelve rooms a bit sparse for a lord and his retinue of servants – up to thirty in some cases. Public rooms for receiving people and entertaining took up all the space, leading the prolific letter-writer Horace Walpole to remark that the nobility in town lived in 'a dining room, a dark back room...and a closet'.

This encouraged outdoor life, and inspired interior designers and architects, such as the Scottish brothers Robert and James Adam, to create the illusion of space indoors. Through-rooms with vistas, alcoves and domes gave a sense of space, and in time the leading makers of pottery would create mock Greek and Roman vases and wall ornaments to provide a relatively inexpensive, ersatz sense of grandeur. It was never easy, however, to keep up with ever-changing fashions. The masterpiece of the Adam brothers, the Adelphi terrace off the Strand, was a commercial disaster because it was finished in the 1770s when the West End had moved away from the river. Few architects or builders in the boom periods escaped the danger of lurching movements in fashion, which might leave them high and dry with a half-built terrace and the building lease still to pay off.

Many contemporaries complained about the poor quality of the rows of terraces put up in the second half of the eighteenth century: if a landlord wanted housing built quickly to cash in on the leases, he would not be too fastidious about the building materials used. A new Building Act in 1774 brought in some control, laying down the basic requirements for houses to be classed according to how much they cost and their size. 'First rate' houses were worth £850 or more, and were the largest; 'fourth rate' houses had a value of less than £150, and were the smallest. Nevertheless, the aim of the landlord and builder was to achieve the impression of opulence at the least cost. This was reflected in the design of Georgian housing, where the façade would give the impression that a terrace of town houses was one grand mansion. Bedford Square, built in the 1770s, remains a fine example. Where there was no such illusion, the row upon row of flat-fronted terraces put up by speculative builders struck many people as visually monotonous in contrast to the higgledy-piggledy appearance of the medieval city.

In the more exclusive squares and streets, monotonous architecture could be relieved by yet another bit of Georgian fakery, Coade stone. Some mystery still surrounds the origin of this very high-quality, durable material, somewhere between earthenware and porcelain, which was moulded into statues and decorative friezes that were widely used in London and all over the world. It was made in a factory established in 1769 by Eleanor Coade, formerly a linen draper, on the south bank of the Thames, where the much later County Hall used to be. Mrs Coade's daughter, also called Eleanor, took over the business from her mother and is generally credited with its success. Coade stone not only had an astonishing durability in the acid air of the city, but it could be cast in moulds, which were created by a talented mason known as John Bacon the elder.

Just how much Coade stone survives is uncertain because it so resembles real stone that it is not easy to identify, but the lion on the south side of Westminster

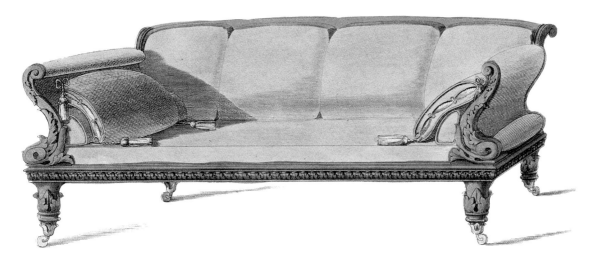

Bridge is made of it, as are many of the decorative features in Bedford Square. After Eleanor Coade's death in 1821, production continued for another twenty years, but the moulds were sold in 1843, and no more was made, though the supposedly secret formula of Coade stone is now known.

An elegant canapé sofa advertised in the London Cabinet Maker and Upholsterer's Guide for 1826. Pieces like this were strongly influenced by the contemporary French Neoclassical style, and were produced throughout the nineteenth century.

Prominent architects and designers of the Georgian period, such as Robert and James Adam, were employed to transform houses both inside and out. These elaborately swagged curtains would have been designed to coordinate with the room's wall covering and furniture.

115

CONSUMER SOCIETY

Despite its own increasing industrialisation, London never ceased to be a huge and ever-growing consumer market that fuelled and fed the newly established industries in the Midlands and the north of England. Other towns grew, or grew up, at a greater speed between the 1760s and the early Victorian period: the hurriedly constructed and insanitary dormitory terraces of the mills; the great centres of the cotton trade – Manchester and Liverpool; Birmingham – the capital of the toyware industries (buttons and buckles)...in fact, any city linked to new manufactures grew apace. Places devoted to leisure, such as Bath and Brighton, watering-holes for the wealthy, also enjoyed a boom. But London remained pre-eminent as the centre of fashion. No ambitious industrialist could ignore its power to make or break his fortune.

All the mill-wheels driven by wind, water or steam, all the see-sawing beam engines drawing water from the mines where coal, clay or tin was hacked out, all

the spinning bobbins in the new factories had arisen and prospered because they were, for the most part, making things you could buy in the shops. The new industrialists competed with London craftsmen, who had the advantage of working close to the centre of fashion, but who could be beaten on price by the mechanised factories of the Midlands and the North. The London shops themselves were new, gradually replacing the market fairs and the travelling salesmen or 'packmen', who travelled the country laden with pots and pans. And as the demand for goods widened, there arose for the first time widespread national advertising carried in newly established newspapers, which could be sent around the country on stagecoaches, picking up speed as new roads were built.

Before the advent of shops as we know them today, most wares were sold by travelling salesmen, or at market stalls in the towns. This stallholder is selling children's toys and pictures.

116

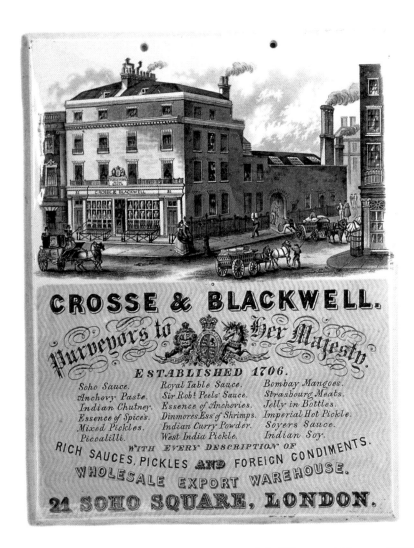

Left: Crosse & Blackwell, established in Soho in 1706, satisfied a new taste for preserved foods. These premises were an early example of a shop as we would recognise it today.

Right: Printing presses such as this were responsible for the spread of newspapers, which, in turn, carried advertisements for fashionable goods, and thus contributed to the growth of industry.

Although the pace of change quickened after 1800, all the signs of it were evident in the last years of the eighteenth century. In 1786 a German lady novelist (perhaps the first) shipped across the North Sea from Holland to Harwich, and hired a post-chaise to take her to London in style, though she envied the bustling camaraderie of the mail coach she saw at Colchester. Once in her lodgings, Sophie von la Roche ventured out with her grown-up son, Carl, into the teeming streets of London's West End, and was dazzled by what she saw. The fashionable streets seemed to stretch for miles, and she wrote home:

Fabric manufacturers and wholesalers could submit their latest patterns to the Repository of Arts... magazine. If the swatches displayed sufficient 'novelty, fashion and elegance', the magazine would order them in quantity and sell them direct to its readers.

We strolled up lovely Oxford Street this evening, for some goods look more attractive by artificial light. Just imagine, dear children, a street taking half an hour to cover from end to end, with double rows of brightly shining lamps, in the middle of which stands an equally long row of beautifully lacquered coaches... First one passes a watchmakers, then a silk or fan store, now a silversmith's, a china or glass shop... Most of all we admired a stall with Argand and other lamps...every variety of lamp, crystal, lacquer and metal ones... The highest lord and humble labourer may purchase here lamps of immense beauty and price or at a very reasonable figure... I stayed long enough to notice this, and was pleased with a system which supplied the common need – light – in this spot, whether for guineas or for pence, so efficiently.

Twenty years before Sophie von la Roche arrived in London, the forest of old tradesmen's signs that cluttered the shopping streets had been removed by law: they had become unsightly and often hazardous. If a shoemaker's sign fell on your head, it could kill. Now, in the 1780s, it was the shop windows that lured in the customers. Frau von la Roche wrote:

We especially noticed a cunning device for showing women's materials. Whether they are silks, chintzes or muslins, they hang down in folds behind fine high windows so that the effect of this material or that material, as it would be in the ordinary folds of a woman's dress, can be studied... Behind great glass windows absolutely everything one can think of is neatly, attractively displayed, and in such an abundance of choice as almost to make one greedy...

A London fabric
shop, Harding &
Howell of Pall Mall,
in 1809, when
cotton fabrics had
become fashionable.

The 'idle rich' had the
money and leisure to
change their clothes
several times a day.
These illustrations
from 1827 show what
women of fashion
would have worn
at breakfast and in
the evening.

ENGLISH CHINAWARE

Northern manufacturers who wanted to expand their market understood that they had to get into London. Royal patronage could be the key to a fortune, and a big London showroom would attract the growing middle-class market of lawyers, bankers and merchants. Among the many products pouring out of the factories of industrial Britain for which the world was greedy was the wonderful new range of pottery – vases, plates, cups and decorative china of all kinds. There were, by 1786, a number of well-known brand names, but one above all others was on the lips of those in pursuit of the latest fashions. On 9 September Sophie von la Roche noted: 'At Wedgwood's to-day I saw a thousand lovely forms and images; vases, tea-things, statuettes, medallions, seals, table-ware and a service on which pictures of the finest villas and gardens of the last three reigns were painted; were I a traveller of means this would have accompanied me home to Germany.'

By that time you could buy Wedgwood pottery in Germany, and, in fact, in a great many countries around the world, for what had begun as a small-scale business in the old Potteries district of Staffordshire in 1754 had become an international business with huge profits. The man who achieved this, with considerable assistance from his partners, was Josiah Wedgwood. Born in 1730 in Burslem, Staffordshire, he was the youngest child of a large family: it is not quite certain if he had eleven or twelve brothers and sisters. The Wedgwoods had been potters for several generations, and Josiah was destined to spend his life at the wheel, shaping the rough stoneware that supplied a mostly local market.

Wedgwood knew very well from his background that there was a great deal more to making pots than throwing clay. He came of age in a time when, as one historian has put it, a craze for Chinese porcelain swept across Europe, amounting to a kind of 'china mania'. No one outside China knew the formula, but the discovery of some porcelain-manufacturing secrets had produced German Meissen ware of a quality that surpassed anything previously known, and later the French had created something similar at Sèvres. Holland, meanwhile, was turning out painted earthenware made at Delft, and England was producing a kind of soft-paste porcelain. In comparison with Meissen and Sèvres china, most Staffordshire ware looked primitive, clumsy and old-fashioned. However, the search for the right formula to produce true porcelain was already under way.

Whereas European makers of fine and extremely expensive porcelain were subsidised and sponsored by royalty, English manufacturers struggled unaided to make ends meet selling on the open market. Most of them, based in London rather than the traditional home of pottery in Staffordshire, went bankrupt. Their crockery was simply too expensive. What was needed to satisfy the tastes of the house-proud, newly emerging middle class of the later eighteenth century was an alternative to true porcelain that was regarded as high quality, fashionable and affordable. This is what Josiah Wedgwood initially set out to achieve.

When he was twenty-four years old, Wedgwood went into partnership with a well-respected and moderately successful potter called Thomas Whieldon, who had a factory at Fenton Vivian, near Stoke. After five years with Whieldon, Wedgwood set up on his own. It took long hours of painstaking and often frustrating experimentation with clays and glazes before he found a way of creating his own distinctive,

An example of one of Josiah Wedgwood's brilliant deceptions – jasperware. Coarsely ground jasper (opaque quartz) was dipped in a film of finely ground material to give an apparently fine finish. To keep the secret of its creation, Wedgwood spread a rumour that it was made from American Cherokee clay.

decorative pottery that could compete with the craze for porcelain *chinoiserie*. Having achieved this, the problem then remained of how to produce the wares quickly and in sufficient quantity. The first part of the problem was solved by the invention of 'transfer printing', in which a pattern created on an engraved copper plate could be transferred to earthenware. The second part was resolved by going into partnership with a Leeds firm that hand-decorated pottery.

On one of his visits to his transfer printers, Sadler & Green of Liverpool, Josiah fell ill. The doctor who visited him brought along a friend, Thomas Bentley. He and Wedgwood struck up an immediate friendship, which was to last from that first meeting in 1762 until Bentley's death in 1780. They wrote to each other constantly, the cultured and well-travelled Bentley opening up for Wedgwood a whole world of fashionable taste. In fact, Wedgwood described Bentley's letters to him (all, sadly, now lost) as 'my magazines, reviews, chronicles & I had almost say my Bible'. But he and Bentley did not become business partners straight away: it was not until 1767 that Bentley signed an agreement to join him as 'Vase maker General'. He, along with Sarah Wedgwood, a distant cousin whom Josiah married in 1764, went on to be great influences on the business.

Makers of fashionable goods could never ignore the London market. The celebrated ceramicist Josiah Wedgwood had several showrooms in the capital, including this one in York Street, off St James's Square, which was managed by his nephew and partner Tom Byerley. This illustration dates from 1809, fifteen years after Wedgwood's death.

All the wonderful array of Wedgwood that Sophie von la Roche had admired on her visit to the company's showrooms in Greek Street, just twenty years after Josiah teamed up with Thomas Bentley, was the result of astonishing and sustained enterprise. A factory, which Wedgwood called Etruria, employed all the latest equipment and enabled him to achieve something approaching mass-production. He campaigned for new turnpike roads on which he could transport his crockery in horse-drawn wagons instead of the lines of

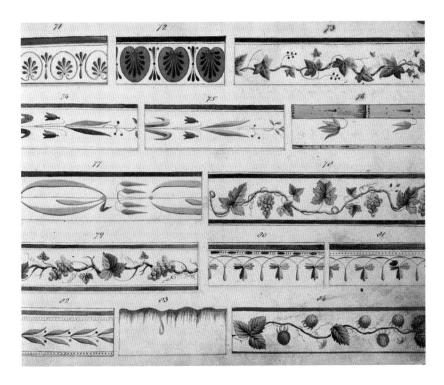

New printing techniques made the mass-production of elegant ceramic tableware possible. This page from the first Wedgwood pattern book (issued in the 1770s) includes the popular Blue Shell Edge and the traditional Grape & Vine border.

packhorses and packmen who had traditionally carried pottery on rough tracks from Staffordshire to the river ports. He was a partner in the building of the Duke of Bridgewater's canal, and an enthusiast in the canal mania that followed. He recognised that he needed London showrooms to attract fashionable clientele, and he was brilliant at promotion: 'Fashion is infinitely superior to merit in many respects' was one of his sayings, though he never let his standards drop or made really cheap goods.

One of Wedgwood's first commercial successes was an order that came in by a round-about route from Queen Charlotte for a 'complete set of tea things, with a gold ground and raised flowers upon it in green'. The order had been picked up by his brother John, who was based in London and had become his agent. The pottery was called 'creamware', but Josiah re-named it 'Queens ware', and found that it was in tremendous demand once it was known that it had been bought by royalty. His talent for turning clays into a dazzling array of decorated ceramics displayed in glittering London showrooms made him a fortune, and his success story is a classic of the Industrial Revolution.

Dating from 1770 to 1780, these matching tureens in cream-coloured earthenware are decorated with a hand-painted 'antique' border. Queen Charlotte's liking for this type of crockery led to Wedgwood renaming it 'Queen's Ware'.

123

TOYWARE

A leading light of the new industrialism, remembered now chiefly for his partnership with James Watt in the manufacture of improved steam engines, was Matthew Boulton. He was one of the sharpest businessmen of his day, his Soho works in Birmingham turning out an astonishing array of buttons, buckles and fancy accoutrements made of various metals, which were sold not only in London but around the world. (His machines could be adapted to make different products, which is why James Watt first approached him to make parts for steam engines.) Nobody was more fashion-conscious than Boulton, who introduced the idea, copied by Wedgwood, of anticipating the demand for 'toys' – as his manufactures were then called – occasioned by some royal event. He and others dreaded a royal death and its compulsory period of bleak mourning because, though it might be a boom time for the carvers of jet mourning jewellery, it temporarily suppressed the fashionable trades.

The pattern books of Boulton and his partner John Fothergill show that in 1772 they had no fewer than 1470 designs for sword hilts, scabbard mounts, buckles, buttons, watch-guards and a bewildering array of other trinkets and jewels, including the false-gold ornaments known as pinchbecks, supposedly after the deviser of the metal, Christopher Pinchbeck. The Soho factory turned out plated metal tankards, cups, coffee pots, jugs, candlesticks, sauce boats, terrines, saucepans, cheese toasters, sugar basins, 'all manner of chimney piece ornaments, intirely gilt in Or Moulu'. Ormulu, as it is now spelt, literally 'ground gold', was made with copper, zinc and tin and used as a mock-gold gilding on a great variety of decorative objects. Only the French knew how to make it until Boulton, with a few bribes, extracted the secret and began production around 1768. He introduced it to the London market with sales at Christie's auction rooms.

A typical steel and jasperware buckle produced around 1750 by Matthew Boulton. The cameo was made by Josiah Wedgwood.

Although the export trade was always important for Boulton and Fothergill, they were keen watchers of London fashion, and creators of it, if they were lucky. 'Fashion has much to do in these things,' Boulton wrote to a friend in 1772, 'and that of the present age distinguishes itself by adopting the most elegant ornaments without presuming to invent new ones.' Whether he was making toyware for the English nobility, the Americans or the Greeks, he stuck to his principles of 'elegant simplicity'. Boulton had his own museum of objects copied for his decorations, including the heads of deer, rams and lions.

In much the same way as the makers of sportswear today seek the endorsement of footballers or other sporting stars, so Boulton and Fothergill contrived to stick their buttons on the most influential aristocrats. The *Gentleman's Magazine* began to take an interest in royal birthdays from the 1760s, and the Soho foundry could advertise its commemorative buttons marking the monarch's birthday. Boulton occasionally used cameos made by Wedgwood to decorate his buttons and buckles. He also personally presented his work to royalty, or had his representatives call on them. When advertisements for his wares appeared in the papers, he spent hours studying them in coffee-houses.

Boulton's attention to the London market was meticulous. Like Wedgwood, he did not want any riff-raff attending exhibitions of his work, and was keen to make sure James Christie, the former naval midshipman who founded the famous auction rooms in 1766, kept the clientele exclusive. Christie advised holding sales during the London season, preferably at Easter, before everyone disappeared to the countryside. On his visits to London Boulton stayed with the very cream of society, and satisfied their tastes for ornament, making many decorative pieces for the Adam brothers.

However, Boulton clearly understood the profits that could be made from a mass market. In 1794, looking back on his career, he wrote: 'We think it of far more consequence to supply the people than the nobility only; and though you speak contemptuously of hawkers, pedlars and those who supply petty shops, yet we must own that we think they will do more towards supporting a great manufactory, than all the lords in the nations...' He sought the patronage of royalty and the first circle of society principally to increase his sales, which he did, adorning countless moderately prosperous Georgian houses with well-made, but affordable, clocks, pots and trinkets.

SHORTAGE OF MONEY

Astonishing as it may seem, throughout the period of tremendous economic growth in the second half of the eighteenth century, the very thing that made the world go round – money – was in a shocking state of neglect. Much of the coinage that changed hands in the pleasure gardens and shops of London was fake – two-thirds of it, according to some estimates. The Royal Mint produced such poorly struck silver and copper coins that they were easily imitated or recycled from shavings that were then remoulded. A reasonable supply of gold coins was minted, but there was a farcical shortage of the lower-value copper and silver currency used in day-to-day business. Without this cash, Samuel Oldknow, a Lancashire cotton manufacturer, found it impossible to pay his workforce, so his relatives would send him whatever money they could garner hidden in bundles of cloth. Oldknow tried everything to get hold of cash: he even went into retailing. Finally, he gave his workforce 'shop notes' with which they could buy what they needed from company shops. This so-called 'truck' system became widespread because of the shortage of coinage.

The situation became so desperate that tokens were struck, which were not illegal if they did not attempt to copy the official currency. The shortfall was partially plugged by foreign silver coins and specially issued banknotes; but the Anglesey Copper Company indulged in a fine bit of free enterprise by using high-grade ore to produce what was called the 'Druid penny', which had the same value as the officially minted coin. By the time the government took action, the official currency from the Royal Mint had become relatively insignificant in daily commerce.

The currency chaos inspired Boulton to go into striking coins himself, using his expertise and the hired skills of engravers drawn from several countries. What he produced could not easily be copied, as it incorporated anti-counterfeiting innovations, such as edge lettering and relief designs. In 1797, after a good deal of lobbying, he was commissioned by the government to produce 45 million penny and twopenny pieces. This he did with a steam-driven engine and a form of mass-production in which a metal strip went into one end of the machine and coins emerged at the other: all the cutting and decoration was achieved 'in line'. In that same year Boulton was commissioned by Catherine the Great to re-equip the Russian mint, while his Soho works remained responsible for much of the British coinage. Boulton & Watt steam-powered minting machines were supplied to Spain, Denmark, Mexico and India.

A fearless man, Boulton dealt harshly with those who tried to steal his coins and those who tried to forge them. He would defend the Soho works with a posse of men wielding blunderbusses, and on one occasion made a night-time raid on forgers, smashing down the doors of their homes and chasing them through the streets. This was when he was in his seventies. At the very end of his life he was commissioned to set up the new Royal Mint at Tower Hill in London, which went into operation in 1810, one year after his death (and continued to produce coins until 1975). In the end, Boulton, whose Birmingham Soho works had adorned so much of the fashionable world in his lifetime, made money out of making money. And some of the money Boulton minted would be spent in the pleasure gardens of London.

PLEASURE GARDENS

It was to the South Bank, across the river and away from the built-up area north of the Thames, that Londoners traditionally took a wherry boat for a day or a night out. The first of the pleasure gardens was in the area known as Vauxhall (a corruption of Foulkes Hall, a country mansion). The New Spring Gardens, as the gardens at Vauxhall were originally known, were an attraction in the seventeenth century, and one that Samuel Pepys enjoyed. 'It is very cheap going thither,' he noted in his diary for 28 May 1667, 'for a man to spend what he will or nothing, all is one – but to hear the nightingales and other birds, and hear here fiddles and there a harp, and here a jews trump, and here laughing, and there fine people walking, is mighty divertising [*sic*].'

The New Spring Gardens had a long life, and at the height of their popularity in the late eighteenth century became known simply as Vauxhall, by which time there were many spectacular entertainments and an admission fee. It is said that when the nightingales and other birds began to disappear as London grew, men with a talent for imitating birdsong were hidden in the bushes at Vauxhall to sustain the rustic atmosphere. When Westminster Bridge was opened in 1750, the owner of the gardens, Jonathan Tyers, had a road built to Vauxhall, and for the first time visitors arrived by coach rather than by riverboat. A local Lambeth historian noted: '…on the first night of the entertainments beginning, so great was the novelty of visiting that delightful spot in a carriage, that the coaches reached from the gardens to beyond Lambeth Church, which is near a mile.'

A speciality of Vauxhall was the fantastic firework displays, which would have matched, or even overshadowed, the Thames-side pyrotechnics that marked the beginning of the new millennium on the night of 31 December 1999. One of the great Vauxhall attractions of the early nineteenth century was a tightrope walker, who called herself Madame Saqui. She would climb a pole to a tightrope suspended at a slope, the highest point 60 feet in the air, with no safety net below her, and with a stick to help her balance, descended slowly, pirouetting all the way, as fireworks exploded around her. Vauxhall Gardens was still going strong in the 1830s, and was described by A. Thornton in *Don Juan in London* (1836):

> …the gardens are beautiful and extensive, and contain a variety of walks, brilliantly illuminated with variegated coloured lamps and terminated with transparent paintings, the whole disposed with so much taste and effect, as to produce a sensation bordering on enchantment in the visitor…the wonderful aerial ascent of Mme Saqui from the most astonishing height, on a tight rope; an exhibition that again transports

Overleaf: One of the most popular social venues in eighteenth- and early nineteenth- century London was Vauxhall Gardens on the south bank of the Thames. Here people could see and be seen, eat and drink, or watch the various entertainments on offer.

the spectator in imagination to fairy land, since the ease, grace and rapidity with which this lady descends, aided by the light of fireworks that encompass her, and still more by the darkness of the surrounding atmosphere, combine to give the appearance of flight of some celestial being...'

In 1742 a rival to Vauxhall was opened on the north bank of the river, close to where the Chelsea Hospital, home to Chelsea Pensioners, now stands. Formerly the residence of Lord Ranelagh, it was bought by theatrical impresarios from Drury Lane Theatre, who turned it into a pleasure garden. It was an instant success, attracting the aristocracy to its huge Rotunda, where meals were served and the London 'quality' could see and be seen. James Boswell, biographer of Samuel Johnson, went there many times for the company and to cheer himself up. On 4 May 1763 he had been traumatised by watching a hanging at Tyburn, but his spirits had returned a week later and he noted in his London diary for 11 May:

> This day I dined at Dempster's. Then dressed and at seven went to Lord Eglington's, and with Mrs Brown and Mrs Reid went in his coach to Ranelagh. I felt a glow of delight entering again that elegant place. This is an entertainment quite peculiar to London. The noble Rotunda all surrounded with boxes to sit in and such a profusion of well dressed people walking round is very fine. My spirits were now better.

Around the walls of the Rotunda were forty-seven boxes for taking refreshments, with doors at the back leading to the gardens. Twenty-three chandeliers hung from the broad ceiling of the dome, which measured 150 feet across at its base. For a while Ranelagh stole Vauxhall's thunder, but it went under much earlier: the Rotunda was demolished in 1805, and the grounds sold off.

A season ticket for Vauxhall Gardens issued to a Mr Wood in 1750. Wealthy pleasure-seekers who went to the gardens frequently could save on the shilling admission fee with these tokens.

THE BALLOON CRAZE

During the 1780s, a new excitement gripped the crowds at the pleasure gardens: ballooning. The first successful manned flight in a hot-air balloon had been made by the French Montgolfier brothers in Paris in 1783. This began a craze that quickly spread to England. English chemists, such as Joseph Priestley and Henry Cavendish, had begun to isolate and name gases that were several times lighter than air, and Cavendish's hydrogen, which could be produced with iron filings and sulphuric acid, became the favoured 'fuel'.

Since nobody was sure what effect sailing thousands of feet in the air would have on living creatures, ducks and dogs were hoisted in baskets. For a while, balloons looked like the transport of the future: Erasmus Darwin tried to send a letter by a miniature balloon, but it landed miles from its intended destination. Balloons of all kinds, made of linen, paper and silk, began to float over cities, to the amazement and amusement of huge crowds. A race to achieve the first manned flight in Britain attracted various contenders, and it is still not clear who won. The following report appeared in the *London Chronicle* with the dateline Edinburgh, Aug 27 1784.

> Mr. Tytler has made several improvements upon his fire balloon. The reason of its failure formerly was its being made of porous linen, through which the air made its escape. To remedy this defect, Mr. Tytler has got it covered with a varnish to retain the inflammable air after the balloon is filled.
>
> Early this morning this bold adventurer took his first aerial flight. The balloon being filled at Comely Garden, he seated himself in the basket, and the ropes being cut he ascended very high and descended quite gradually on the road to Restalrig, about half a mile from the place where he rose, to the great satisfaction of those spectators who were present. Mr. Tytler went up without the furnace this morning; when that is added he will be able to feed the balloon within flammable air, and continue his aerial excursions as long as he chooses.
>
> Mr. Tytler is now in high spirits, and in his turn laughs at those infidels who ridiculed his scheme as visionary and impracticable. Mr. Tytler is the first person in Great Britain who has navigated the air.

Next to nothing is known about Tytler, whose flight was brief and not without incident: his first balloon of linen was not airtight, and on one occasion his basket caught fire. A much better publicised and authenticated ascent is that of Vincent Lunardi, an Italian, who, in 1784, was based in London as secretary to the

Neapolitan ambassador. Lunardi's balloon was first exhibited at the Lyceum Theatre, and he got permission to fly from the grounds of Chelsea Hospital. But before Lunardi was ready, a Frenchman named Dr Moret tried to steal his thunder by launching his balloon from Ranelagh Pleasure Gardens, which adjoined Chelsea Hospital. Moret had raised a good deal of subscription money to finance his flight, and when his balloon failed to take off, he disappeared, leaving behind an angry crowd. Lunardi had to find a new launch pad, which was provided by the Royal Artillery Company at Moorfields.

On 15 September 1784 a huge crowd gathered to witness Lunardi's historic flight in his beautiful red and white silk balloon, which would be lifted into the sky by hydrogen. The Prince of Wales observed from close quarters, gaining a good view of the balloon's comical undercarriage, to which oars had been attached for steering. The tension mounted when the balloon failed to lift Lunardi and his passenger, plus a cat, a dog and some pigeons, into the air. A lighter basket was fitted and the passenger jettisoned. This did the trick, and the balloon rose to the gasps of the crowd. Royal observers watched with telescopes as the balloon sailed above London, and Lunardi, rowing frantically and ineffectively with his oars, was

Ballooning became all the rage after the pioneer flight of Vincent Lunardi from the Royal Artillery Ground at Moorfields in London on 15 September 1784. Lunardi tried to steer his hydrogen balloon with paddles, but they were ineffective. He ended up miles from London, at the village of Ware in Hertfordshire.

the first to see the great metropolis laid out below. To calm his nerves he drank some wine and chewed on a cooked chicken leg. An oar broke, a pigeon fluttered off, and still the balloon continued to rise. In fact, it got so high that ice began to form on the ropes of the balloon and the cat shivered uncontrollably.

Somehow Lunardi, sailing out into the countryside towards the town of Ware in Hertfordshire, managed to get his balloon down. He thought he achieved this by paddling his oar; others believed that it was thanks to gas escaping. He landed in a field and managed to drop off the frozen cat, which was allegedly grabbed and sold instantly by one of the women who watched Lunardi's craft drag along the ground before rising again. According to the recorded testimony of one witness, the field in which he landed was known locally as Etna, after the volcano in Sicily, because it was used for burning rubbish. As he rose away from the startled farmworkers, he spoke to them through a silver trumpet. When he finally came down again, Lunardi had great difficulty persuading the farmworkers to grab his ropes. He was reported in the *Morning Post* as saying:

> At twenty minutes past four I descended in a meadow near Ware. Some labourers were at work in it. I requested their assistance, but they exclaimed they would have nothing to do with one who came on the Devil's horse, and no entreaties could prevail on them to approach me. I at last owed my deliverance to a young woman in the field who took hold of a cord I had thrown out, and, calling to the men, they yielded that assistance at her request which they had refused to mine.

A 'crude monument' was put up in Ware, commemorating the happy ending of Lunardi's flight, which lasted two hours and fifteen minutes. It seems to have disappeared because the locals have recently discussed putting up a commemorative plaque, though there is some disagreement about whether or not it is right for a community that is troubled by Stansted Airport to show such respect for the first manned flight in England.

Although balloonists were soon crossing the Channel in both directions, the unsteerable aircraft were of no practical use for transport. But they did, for the first time, give map-makers a birds-eye view of the rapidly growing metropolis. Panoramas of London drawn from high above the capital in the first decades of the nineteenth century would show the great dock basin carved out in the east, and to the west the new Regency estates. And at night, in parts of the West End, there were the flickers of much brighter lights than those that had so entranced Sophie von la Roche in 1786.

GASLIGHT

The young American merchant Joseph Ballard, who visited London in 1815, noted in his journal:

> At night a good many of the streets and stores are lighted up with gas. The brilliancy of light thrown out this way is astonishing; compared with it the oil lamps look like a 'dim candle at noon'. It is prepared in some building erected for its purpose and conducted through the streets in pipes like an aqueduct, consequently all the proprietors have to do is to turn a cock and apply a candle and the house or street is lighted.

Matthew Boulton lived just long enough to witness the first tentative flickering of this invention, devised in the last few years of the eighteenth century by his most talented, if eccentric, engineer, William Murdoch (see page 94). Strangely, Boulton, with other projects on his mind, appears to have taken little interest in Murdoch's gas experiments, and missed the chance to take the lead in this novel industry.

In 1779 Murdoch had been sent to Redruth in Cornwall to install Boulton & Watt steam engines, which were in great demand in the mines. It was here he built and showed his working model of a steam carrriage, and was involved in many innovations in the workings of steam engines. There is a widespread view that Murdoch's talents were deliberately played down by his employers, but he did well enough for himself and enjoyed freedom to experiment. Sometime in 1792 he had the idea of using the gas given off by coal when heated in an enclosed cylinder as a form of lighting. But, as with all inventions, there are rival claimants to this far-reaching invention. Chief among them was the French engineer Philippe Lebon, who patented a 'thermolamp' in 1799. This was simply a glass bowl containing wood shavings that, when heated, gave off a gas, which was lit as it emerged from a thin tube. Lebon wrote a paper predicting that his gas device, with some adaptation, could be used not only to light rooms and streets, but would replace coal fires and ovens, and even heat the bath water. There was just one big snag – his gas had a hideous smell.

Murdoch was probably technically ahead of Lebon when, in 1794, he devised his first primitive lighting system with coal heated in a kettle and drawn off through a pipe made from a gun barrel. Lebon had the vision, but Murdoch had the rigorous mentality of the engineer. He experimented with different lengths of pipe, with ways of storing the gas, with washing it in water to remove the smell, and with the shape of the flame produced, which was dependent on the perforations in the outlet that was lit. By 1798 Murdoch was experimenting with a lighting system at Boulton's Soho factory, though the technical problems of producing a constant and even glow were frustrating.

In 1801 Lebon, by then using gas given off from heated oil, lit up part of the Hotel Seignaly in Paris, both inside and outside. It was a public demonstration seen by James Watt's son Gregory, who reported back to Soho that Murdoch had better get a move on. Another in the audience was a German, Friedrich Winzer, who promptly copied Lebon's lamp. In 1803 he crossed the Channel, Anglicised his name to Frederick Winsor, and gave gaslight demonstrations at the Lyceum Theatre, Covent Garden, which put on a variety of entertainment. (This theatre had displayed Lunardi's balloon, and was also the site of Madame Tussaud's first London exhibition, in 1802.) Winsor then set about lobbying Parliament with a scheme for street gas lighting.

In 1802 the signing of the Peace of Amiens, which brought the war with France to a temporary end, was celebrated all over the country with illuminations and firework displays. Not to be outdone, Boulton had the Soho works bejewelled with lights depicting a female figure giving thanks, a star and the letters GR (for George III). At least some of those lights burnt Murdoch's gas, but it is likely that most were oil lamps, for the new technology was not yet sophisticated enough to produce such an effect. Although Frederick Winsor continued to promote his cause, lighting Carlton House Terrace for the Prince Regent and part of Pall Mall in 1807, it took several years before all the practical problems of replacing oil lamps in the streets were ironed out. Although Murdoch had lit a cotton mill, presaging the horrors of twenty-four-hour working, the Soho factory pulled out of gas altogether in 1814, leaving the field to others.

Gas lighting came in bit by bit, until the London Gas Light and Coke Company finally got a charter in 1812 to light Westminster, Southwark and the City of London. The works were in Great Peter Street, Westminster, and it was not long before Westminster Bridge was gas-lit. By that time, James Boswell was long dead, but gas lighting would have cramped his style, as it did the footpads and other nocturnal criminals in the city.

The first big new development that sought to include all the latest mod cons for its tenants, who would be of the very grandest kind, was Belgravia. Working under commissioners, the development was the masterwork of the remarkable Thomas Cubitt, who had begun life as a humble carpenter. Cubitt was born in 1788, the son of a Norfolk farmer and carpenter, who died when he was a boy. Following two and a half years working as a ship's carpenter on the run to India, he set up in London and rapidly developed a new kind of building business, taking

A street lamp with a brilliant glow lights up the Royal Mail coach in Lombard Street in the City in 1827. Gas lights, which replaced the old oil lamps, were then still a novelty in London and much valued as a guard against crime.

on large contracts and subcontracting all the labour himself. He created a large workshop and impressed developers with the speed and quality of his work.

When he came to develop Belgravia in the 1820s, one of the biggest problems was the laying down of all the basic services. By that time a large part of London's water supply came from new companies that had set up along the Thames and pumped out river water with steam-driven machinery. The new abundance of running water in the better homes encouraged the installation of water closets that had to be flushed. Formerly toilets discharged into cesspits, which were emptied by 'night soil' men. For the water closet to function there had to be a sewer, but there were no sewage treatment works, so the effluent of Belgravia – and Buckingham Palace, on which Cubitt also worked – was discharged straight into the river. This quickly killed the Thames as a salmon river, and by the 1850s the disgusting state of its water forced the Victorians to find a solution.

And then there was the problem of lighting Belgravia. Cubitt naturally wanted gas, so pipes were laid and lampposts put up to his own design and that of George

The view from Regent's Circus, now known as Piccadilly Circus, down Lower Regent Street to Carlton House in 1822. The whole of Regent Street was designed as a fashionable shopping mall, and became very popular with the upper crust from the new West End.

Bavesi, who was involved in the development, but at first there was no supply. Temporary oil lamps had to be put up, much to the annoyance of the early tenants. There were squabbles too over the number of lamps in the street. In 1836 a wealthy banker, H. R. Hoare, who was one of the first residents of Eaton Square, wrote indignantly to the lighting committee when it was suggested that a lamp could be dispensed with.

> [This would] involve encreased encouragement to vice, theft and various other nuisances…which I flattered myself when first becoming one of the early emigrants to this new settlement were provided against and great indeed will be my disappointment after a residence and expenditure for rates etc for many years to find that my person and property have every prospect of being consigned to jeopardy.

Street lighting had become a lively issue. From the 1820s onwards, the old oil lamps disappeared, and London was lit up brighter than ever before. The culmination of the growth of the capital as the brightest and most vibrant city in Europe was the carving out in the 1820s of a brand new shopping street.

REGENT'S PARK AND REGENT STREET

Unique in London's long history of piecemeal, speculative building was the creation of Regent's Park as an aristocratic suburb, and the imposing thoroughfare of Regent Street, which led south from Oxford Circus to Piccadilly, the Haymarket and Carlton House Terrace. The park was a government project supervised by the Commissioners for Woods and Forests, and overseen by the architect John Nash, a favourite of the Prince Regent. The original intention was that only people on horseback should be allowed into the park, which was built on open fields, with the Regent's Canal passing along its northern edge. Regent Street itself, which for the first few years had colonnades to protect shoppers from the rain, cut through a swathe of old building along what had been Swallow Street, and was built as a deliberate barrier between the new West End and the artisans of Soho to the east. At the junctions with Marylebone Road and Oxford Street the plan was to create circuses to add to the grandeur of the scheme, but none of this was finished.

Work on this huge project began in 1816, and tenancies were being taken up in the new shopping parade by 1819. The design of Regent Street, to which many architects other than Nash contributed, broke with the Georgian past. After an uncertain start, it became a huge success, and for a long time was the most popular shopping street in London.

CHAPTER FIVE
A Remedy for Quacks

In a letter home in 1717, Lady Mary Wortley Montagu, who was living in Constantinople as wife of the British ambassador to Turkey, wrote:

> A propos of distempers, I am going to tell you a thing, that will make you wish yourself here. The small-pox, so fatal, and so general amongst us, is here entirely harmless, by the invention of engrafting, which is the term they give it. There is a set of old women, who make it their business to perform the operation, every autumn, in the month of September, when the great heat is abated… Every year, thousands undergo this operation, and the French Ambassador says pleasantly, that they take the small-pox here by way of diversion, as they take the waters in other countries. There is no example of any one that has died in it… I am patriot enough to take the pains to bring this useful invention into fashion in England, and I should not fail to write to some of our doctors very particularly about it, if I knew any one of them that I thought had virtue enough to destroy such a considerable branch of their revenue…

Lady Mary was then twenty-eight years old, the mother of two young children. The discovery that there was a simple way of protecting them against smallpox, the most virulent and feared affliction of the age, which killed and maimed tens of thousands in epidemic years in England, was a revelation. Five years earlier, in 1712, when she was first married, one of her brothers had died of smallpox, and not long afterwards she had been stricken herself and survived. She knew that she was immune, as nobody who had been infected with smallpox caught it again; servants who had survived the disease were especially sought after as they could attend the sick if a household came down with the disease. It was therefore without any fear that she ventured into the poor districts of Constantinople to see the Greek ladies perform their cure.

People send to one another to know if any of their family has a mind to have the small-pox; they make parties for this purpose, and when they are met (commonly fifteen or sixteen together) the old woman comes with a nut-shell full of the matter of the best sort of small-pox, and asks what vein you please to have opened. She immediately rips open that you offer to her, with a large needle (which gives you no more pain than a common scratch) and puts into the vein as much matter as can lie upon the head of her needle, and after that, binds up the little wound with a hollow bit of shell, and in this manner opens four or five veins.

A Gillray cartoon of 1802 depicts the 'wonderful effects of vaccination'. Although there were some fears that taking medicine from a cow could be harmful, Jenner's new vaccines were regarded as a kind of wonder drug to protect against smallpox.

141

INOCULATION AGAINST DISEASE

What Lady Mary called 'engrafting' – a term borrowed from horticulture, and meaning much the same thing – became known as 'inoculation'. In the eighteenth century it was practised only as a means of protecting against smallpox. There were no inoculations for any of the other viral diseases, such as scarlet fever or diphtheria, which inflicted misery on children, and absolutely no understanding of what a virus was – the term simply meant an infectious poison. Smallpox was known to doctors as 'variola', which means 'mottled' or 'spotty', for the victims were covered in hundreds, or even thousands, of hideous pustules which, if they survived, often left them blind, pock-marked or maimed (see 'Blind Jack' Metcalf and Josiah Wedgwood, pages 90 and 144).

There was no scientific theory to explain why the engrafting of smallpox on to the skin of the arm or forehead was likely to induce a mild dose of the disease, which then gave immunity to further attacks. Absolutely nothing was understood about the body's immune system. Engrafting was, essentially, a folk medicine, which had been practised from time to time in Britain, and was based simply on the observation that one attack of smallpox provided immunity. For someone like Lady Mary Wortley Montagu to recommend a procedure against smallpox that had been discovered in Turkey, a country widely regarded as barbaric, was bound to stir up trouble.

But Lady Mary was a spirited aristocrat with no fear of authority: she had eloped with Lord Wortley Montagu, whom she had known for several years, when her cantankerous father arranged for her to marry someone wealthier. Her experience at the hands of the best of the medical profession when she caught smallpox had not left her with great admiration for those learned gentlemen, all fellows of the Royal Society. However, it is quite possible it was on her sick bed that she first heard about inoculation in Turkey. Emmanuel Timoni, a doctor working in Constantinople, had written a paper describing it, which had been published in the transactions of the Royal Society in 1714, and other doctors had given accurate descriptions of the procedure and the generally beneficial results. Nobody had thought to try it in England, however.

Attached to the British Embassy in Constantinople was an English surgeon called Charles Maitland. He had seen engrafting done, but it was with reluctance that he agreed to be present when Lady Mary arranged for her own young son to be inoculated. In an account of this historic episode, Maitland wrote in 1723: 'she…sent for an old Greek woman who had practised in this way for many years…but so awkwardly by the shaking of her hand, put the child to so much torture with her blunt and rusty needle, that I pitied his cries…and therefore inoculated the other arm with my own instrument, and with so little pain to him, that he did not in the least complain of it.'

The 'anything she can do I can do better' tone of Maitland's account must raise suspicions, but this was almost certainly the very beginning of the adoption of inoculation by an English doctor. When, in 1718, the Wortley Montagus returned to London, Lady Mary requested Maitland, who had returned to his country practice, to inoculate her daughter. He was uneasy about this, but he agreed to it and had medical observers along to witness the procedure. Word of the successful inoculation spread, and Princess Caroline, daughter-in-law of George I, asked the King for permission to inoculate her children. First there was a test done on six criminals awaiting the scaffold in Newgate Prison. They all survived and were rewarded for their role in medical experimentation with a reprieve. It is said that all but one had had smallpox already, so they were not even risking their lives to escape the gallows. Inoculation of Princess Caroline's daughters, but not her sons, went ahead, again without mishap.

INOCULATION IN BRITAIN

Gradually, the resistance of the medical profession was broken down. But very soon the adoption of inoculation took a course that Lady Mary had feared: the physicians were not prepared to imitate old women, and developed their own disgusting, elaborate and extremely expensive inoculation procedure. The hapless patient was purged, bled and starved for days and weeks beforehand, a ritual the doctors called 'preparation', and the infective matter was inserted into a deep wound cut with a lancet. One doctor recommended cutting almost to the bone, a very dangerous method, as the reason inoculation worked was that infection through the skin gave the patient's immune system time to combat the disease. Lady Mary railed against this medical overkill and had an article published in a paper called the *Flying Post* in which she signed herself 'A Turkey Merchant'.

When Edward Jenner was born in Berkeley, Gloucestershire, on 17 May 1749, cutting to the bone was the standard procedure for those who could afford the 'very best' in smallpox inoculation. Jenner, the eighth of nine children, was just five years old when both his parents died. An older sister, Mary, who was to marry the incoming vicar, became his surrogate mother. When he was about seven years old he was inoculated, an experience that his contemporary biographer said left him traumatised: he had nightmares long after. His experience was far from unique. In some poor parishes the work was done by lay people, often the village blacksmith, because nobody could afford the surgeon's fees.

Undeterred, Jenner went on to study medicine in London under John Hunter, one of the leading surgeons of the day, and younger brother of the eminent anatomist William Hunter. By the time Jenner qualified and returned to Berkeley to practise, there were already changes in inoculation methods. Two surgeons, Robert and Daniel Sutton of Essex, had been very successful with a less elaborate method of inoculation, and by the 1780s had made a good deal of money taking their top-secret system around the country. It was not long before doctors were advertising the new, improved inoculation technique as 'without preparation', as if it were some kind of brilliant advance rather than a correction of their own mistake.

As he went on his rounds in Gloucestershire, including Cheltenham, where poor 'mad' King George III went for his purgings, Jenner practised the Suttonian method: it was becoming routine. Josiah Wedgwood, who had lost a leg to smallpox as a child, had his infant son and daughter inoculated in 1767, though not without some trepidation. He wrote to a friend that the children 'have had a pretty smart pox as our doctor terms it. I believe they have had no dangerous symptoms, but have been so very ill that I confess I repented what we had done…' Yet the Wedgwoods' next child was inoculated and came out of it well. The eminent Dr Erasmus Darwin, who knew Wedgwood from the so-called Lunar Society (a group dedicated to the discussion and propagation of new ideas), was enthusiastic about inoculation.

Jenner, though a respected country doctor, had nothing like Darwin's range of interests or lively correspondence with engineers and scientists. His great interest was in nature, and he was elected to the Royal Society for his observations on young cuckoos, proving that they tipped the eggs of their adoptive parents out of the nest. The Royal Society was not so impressed with his next submission, many years later, in which he presented evidence that he had found a safer way of inoculating against smallpox. His paper, which in another form was to make him world famous, was refused publication in the Society's transactions.

COWPOX VERSUS SMALLPOX

It was common knowledge in Gloucestershire and some other rural districts of England that certain people were immune to smallpox. They included grooms who looked after horses, and dairymaids who milked the cows. How many people had put two and two together and reasoned that what was protecting them was a dose of the disease called cowpox we do not know. A Dorset dairy farmer called Benjamin Jesty had made the connection, and used cowpox rather than smallpox to inoculate his wife and family in 1774. He had not published anything about it, and Jenner did not learn of Jesty's rustic experiment until much later.

There was a question mark, anyway, over how long a cowpox inoculation provided immunity, and Jenner began to gather case histories. Quite often, he discovered, an inoculation would not 'take', and, checking back, Jenner found that the patient had suffered something like cowpox twenty or thirty years previously. That was one part of his dossier sent to the Royal Society. But the key experiment would involve infecting someone with cowpox, leaving them a while, and then inoculating them with smallpox. If the smallpox did not 'take', then the patient had been given immunity with cowpox. This was significant because cowpox was never fatal, whereas inoculation with smallpox itself could, and did, go wrong.

Frustrated by the lack of support he received from the Royal Society, Jenner went to London in 1798 and got his study printed privately. The title was not exactly catchy:

An INQUIRY into the Causes and Effects of Variole Vaccinae
A DISEASE discovered in
some of the Western Counties of England,
particularly Gloucestershire
and known by the name THE COW POX.

A French cartoon telling the story of Edward Jenner's discovery that inoculation with cowpox could protect humans from smallpox. Jenner's term for cowpox, Variola vaccinae, *meaning literally 'smallpox of the cow', gave rise to the terms 'vaccine' and 'vaccination'.*

145

As there was no Latin term for cowpox, he invented one: *Variola vaccinae*, which meant literally 'smallpox of the cow'. Within a year or two the new, safer way of inoculating became known as 'vaccination', to indicate that cowpox rather than smallpox itself was used. Jenner's vaccines were regarded as miracle drugs, and demands for them came in from people all over the world, including President Thomas Jefferson in the United States. Cowpox was quite rare in England, and did not occur at all in America or Ireland, so the problem of supply was acute. Although Jenner did his best to find vaccines, taking some from dairy cattle in London, a search began in Europe for a reliable source. Napoleon had his troops vaccinated, though with what exactly we will never know. The belief that this new way of inoculating was safe and effective gave rise to what one sceptical London doctor called 'cow mania'.

Jenner put in for a reward from Parliament, which was bitterly opposed by other doctors, but he won the day and was eventually handed the equivalent of more than £1 million for his discovery of vaccination. Smallpox was not, however, eliminated, and opposition within the medical profession continued well into the nineteenth century. The controversy was not resolved at the time of Jenner's death in 1823, by which time so much doubt had been cast upon the true value of vaccination that his fame had subsided. The government of the day turned down a request to have him buried in Westminster Abbey, and only a few of his local friends and admirers attended his funeral in the parish church of Berkeley, Gloucestershire, where he was born and lived most of his life.

As a final indignity, a statue of Jenner, which had been placed in Trafalgar Square in London in 1858, was removed four years later and hidden away in a corner of Kensington Gardens, where it remains to this day. Jenner's reputation was revived later in the nineteenth century, when the French chemist Louis Pasteur, searching for a way of protecting against rabies, suggested that all forms of inoculation against infectious diseases should be called vaccination in honour of the English doctor's pioneer work. And when vaccination for many diseases other than smallpox was shown to be effective in the twentieth century, Jenner's star in the firmament of medical history rose further. The pioneering but contentious days of cow mania were forgotten, and the English country doctor was elevated to the ranks of medical genius, and even called the 'father of immunology'.

In many ways, the Jenner story captures, in essence, medical practice during the years of the Industrial Revolution. There was, in reality, no breakthrough in the understanding of infectious diseases, immunology, the importance of vitamins or anything else – that was a century away. But the scientific method, and the will to investigate and test theories, was very strong, and even when understanding was completely lacking and medical fashion was laughably wide of the mark, real advances were made. Jenner's achievement was the more remarkable for the fact that popular medicine was driven by the same kind of consumer boom that saw the mass-production of cotton goods and porcelain. This was not just the era of new crockery: it was, as the medical historian Roy Porter put it, the 'Golden Age of Quackery'. And who was to tell what was a genuine cure and what was useless? After all, the bleeding of patients to cure fevers and improve health was practised by leading doctors, though it killed many of their patients. Even the horribly wounded and those with amputated limbs after the Battle of Waterloo in 1815 were bled, when what they desperately needed was a blood infusion. Yet bleeding by cutting veins or using leeches was still prevalent at the end of the nineteenth century. In fact, leeches are used today in microsurgery, and bleeding is practised for very specific conditions, but in the eighteenth century it was regarded as a cure-all, and was much more harmful than many of the quack potions on sale.

PATENT MEDICINES

Edward Jenner himself hoped he had chanced upon a nice little earner with his own 'stomach medicine', and was encouraged by his teacher and mentor, the eminent London surgeon John Hunter. 'I am puffing your tartar as the tartar of all tartars,' Hunter wrote to Jenner. He had put it out for trial and advised: 'Had you not better let a book-seller have it to sell, as Glass of Oxford did his magnesia? Let it be called "Jenner's Tartar Emetic", or anybody else's that you please.' Booksellers became distributors of the new 'proprietary medicines', and Hunter suggested Jenner try the biggest of them all, John Newbery.

Jenner also had his own 'indigestion lozenges', sold by Savory of London, and when he was attacked for making unfounded claims for the efficacy of his vaccines, the fact that he was quite happy to indulge in what others regarded as 'quackery' was used to undermine his reputation. But the fact of the matter was that most of the leading physicians and surgeons of the day indulged in a bit of medicinal free enterprise, and the formulae of their potions for curing everything from gout to cancer were not necessarily any more medically useful than those of out-and-out charlatans. There were no officially controlled trials of drugs as there are today, and though we can say now that some of them probably did work, the only way to find out in the eighteenth century was by trial and error – on yourself.

Members of the Royal College of Physicians and respected surgeons were not above indulging in their own brand of quackery. Dr James, for example, made a fortune from his 'powders', which sold in their millions in the vibrant medical market of the day.

Although the charge of quackery was aimed continuously at one doctor or pseudo-medic by the others, there was no real conflict between 'regular' medicine and that sold in packets with enticing labels, such as 'The True Spirit of Scurvy-Grass'. This last was advertised as available through the Penny Post, a mail service begun in London in the seventeenth century and later taken over by the government. Many sellers of patent medicines travelled the country, having bills printed to announce their imminent arrival; one asked locals to look out for him in his one-horse 'calico', a kind of convertible carriage that could have its hood up or down.

The customers for these patent powders, elixirs, drops and syrups were not the poorest people, but the emerging middle classes of shopkeepers, clerks, lawyers, and doctors themselves, who could not afford the exorbitant fees charged by visiting physicians. On the whole, what was on offer was not an 'alternative' medicine, but a cheap packaged version of what you were likely to get from the most eminent doctors in Harley Street. This was not the same quackery as prevailed a century earlier when mountebanks drew crowds and offered to cure 'the Glimmering of Gizzard, the Quavering of the Kidneys and the Wombling Trot'. Times had changed, and the definition of ailments was at least more realistic than the earlier roll-call of quackery, satirised as:

Stanton's Pills – among the most popular patent medicines during the eighteenth century.

The Cramp, the Stitch
The Squirt the Itch
The Gout, the Stone, the Pox
The Mulligrubs
The Bonny Scrubs
And all Pandora's Box!

What was on offer in the 1780s, as listed in the *Coventry Mercury*, included Ruston's Pills for Rheumatism, Storey's Worm Cakes, Velno's Vegetable Syrup and Swinfen's Electuary for the Stone and Gravel. Around the country the new stagecoaches, running faster on better roads, carried letters from one sufferer to another recommending this or that powder or drop by which they 'swore'. By the early 1800s the market was huge, and the most successful makers of own-brand medicines made fortunes. For example, Nathaniel Godbold, who was a baker by trade, made £10,000 a year from his Vegetable Balsam, which was supposed to cure venereal disease. An alternative VD cure, which was also advertised as a guard against tuberculosis, was Velno's Vegetable Syrup, which had a murky history before it was bought by a woollen-draper, Isaac Swainson, who earned about £5000 annually from sales of 20,000 bottles. Both Godbold and Swainson made enough to set themselves up in fine country houses, and Swainson became a well-known botanist with his own physic garden.

Although the medicines in themselves were mostly worthless, it was recognised in the eighteenth century that an important influence in any cure was the confidence the patient had in the doctor or the potion they were given. It is what is now called the 'placebo effect', whereby a harmless pill has just as much success in drug control trials as the real thing. The power of suggestion is genuine, even if the pill is phoney. This was demonstrated brilliantly at the very end of the eighteenth century by the Bristol doctor John Haygarth, a meticulous observer of medical cause and effect, and the first to advocate blanket inoculations against smallpox. Haygarth was immune himself to the 'mesmerising' effects of quackery that gripped all sections of society from time to time, and he was responsible for seeing off at least one bogus operator with a neat demonstration of the hollowness of his claims.

The eighteenth century was the golden age of quackery in medicine, and some, such as Isaac Swainson, made a fortune from their branded medicines, most of which were worthless. From the profits of his Velno's Vegetable Syrup, Swainson created a botanic garden that won worldwide fame.

A group of 'mesmerised' French patients painted around 1780. Anton Mesmer caused a sensation in Paris with his 'animal magnetism' cures before he was branded a fraud by physicians. His followers, however, continued to practise mesmerism, which was fashionable for a time in England.

MEDICINE AND MESMER

The term 'mesmerise' is derived from Anton Mesmer who was born in Swabia, now part of southern Germany. Mesmer made a name for himself, and a small fortune in France, with his 'animal magnetism' cures. The rituals he devised strike us now as hilarious, but were believed in implicitly by huge numbers of people in the eighteenth century. Groups of patients holding hands would sit around a tub containing bottles of 'magnetised water' while soft music played in the background. There was a predominance of women among the afflicted, and Mesmer would arrange for his handsome accomplices to massage them, their breasts included, until they reached a pitch of excitement and began to writhe in convulsions. Mesmer would then appear with his own 'magnetic' personality and, when everyone had calmed down, he would claim that he had accomplished a cure-all.

This is the 'Celestial Bed' with which the Scot James Graham offered men a cure for impotence at his Temple of Health in London in 1780. It is said that Lord Nelson's lover Lady Hamilton served her time as one of Graham's thinly clad temple nymphs.

An alternative for men was provided by the 'Celestial Bed' of the Scot James Graham, who opened his Temple of Health in London in 1780, offering an instant cure for impotence. The show included a session in which men were surrounded by thinly clad nymphs as soft music played. How many patients were *really* impotent on arrival at the Temple of Health it is hard to say.

French physicians saw Mesmer off after discrediting his work, but his followers came to England with their own versions of the theory that the world, and people's health, was ruled by magnetic forces. One of these disciples was an American, Elisha Perkins, who had invented what he called 'magnetic tractors'. He died in 1799, but his son, also named Elisha, brought the invention to Denmark and England, founding a Perkinean Institute in London. The 'tractors' consisted of two small pieces of metal, a bit like a tuning fork, which, Perkins claimed, could cure gout, rheumatism, palsy and almost anything

else if moved about on the affected region of the body. Perkins based himself in Leicester Square and began to make a good income from wealthy clients. So that the poor could benefit, a charitable organisation, the Quaker Society of Friends, raised money for a Perkinean Institution, which treated them for free. Perkins himself is said to have amassed a fortune of $50,000 before returning to the United States in 1816.

Haygarth got hold of some of Perkins' patent tractors and had replicas made of wood, but painted to look like metal. When tested by two doctors in a Bath hospital, they had exactly the same effect as the 'real thing', proving beyond doubt that the alleged cures were purely psychosomatic – all in the mind. Haygarth wrote up his findings in *Of the Imagination, as a Cause and Cure of Disorder, exemplified by Fictitious Tractors* (1800). In a desperate effort to save face, the Perkineans tried the tractors on unthinking animals, to no effect, and another fabulous cure bit the dust. In time, however, the methods of the Mesmerists would lead to the development of hypnosis and a better understanding of the power of suggestion in medicine. In exposing a fraud, Haygarth had at the same time made a discovery.

Many quacks became rich by exploiting the desire of sick people for a cure. Among the most notorious was the American Elisha Perkins, whose 'medical tractors' were exposed – amid much embarrassment – as totally fraudulent.

TRIAL, ERROR AND SUCCESS

Real knowledge, and a determination to take an experimental view of medicine, were defining characteristics of the best of eighteenth-century practice, and did sometimes lead to a real breakthrough in treatment. A classic example is the discovery of an effective cure for a horrible disease called dropsy (now known as oedema), which puffed a patient into grotesque shapes and led to a slow death. A contemporary description captured the horror of it: 'Sometimes the liquid – quarts and gallons of it – made arms and legs swell so that they were immovable. Sometimes it poured into the abdomen to form a tremendous paunch. Sometimes it waterlogged the lung cavity and thereby made it impossible for the victim to breathe unless he sat bolt upright all day and all night.'

An age-old treatment for dropsy was a poison derived from the foxglove, which grew wild in the English countryside. It had been named *Digitalis purpurea* in 1542 by the German botanist and physician Leonard Fuchs, who recommended it as a way of 'scattering' the dropsy. Certainly the effects of taking digitalis were well known. Too high a dose and the patient was dead. Even the right dose produced a violent reaction within the body – vomiting, purging, dizziness and weirdly coloured, yellow-green vision. It was because of the dangers of administering digitalis that the treatment was used only intermittently, and more often in folk medicine than by trained doctors. However, it came to the attention of an eminent botanist and physician, William Withering, in the 1770s, and he began a methodical experiment to discover a safe and effective dosage for the treatment of dropsy.

Withering was born in Wellington, Shropshire, in 1741, and studied first at home and then as an apprentice to a local medical practitioner. At the age of twenty-one he enrolled at Edinburgh University, then the top medical establishment, made the obligatory tour of Europe when he had graduated, and settled in Stafford, where he was one of two doctors to be appointed to the new infirmary opened in 1766. Here he fell in love with one of his patients, Helena Cooke, who was an accomplished botanical artist. Withering had plenty of spare time and took up a study of plants in which he had previously shown no interest at all. He invented a special microscope for detailed examination of leaves and seeds, and in 1776 produced a highly respected botanical work, *The Botanical Arrangement of All the Vegetables Growing in Great Britain*. Nothing about the medicinal use of plants was included in the book, and Withering dismissed the 'fables of the ancient herbalists', preferring to start afresh with 'accurate and well considered experiments'.

In the year that his book was published, Withering had moved with his family to Birmingham, 'head-hunted' by Erasmus Darwin, a leading member of the Lunar Society, which Withering soon joined. He returned to Stafford Infirmary once a week to see his old patients, changing horses halfway on the 30-mile journey. As chance would have it, his interest in digitalis as a cure for dropsy was revived by an incident on those weekly trips. During his stop-over en route to Stafford he was asked to attend an elderly lady suffering from a severe case of dropsy. He hung his head and said there was little he could do. On a later trip he enquired how she was and was astonished to learn that she had made a full recovery. The cure was effected by a herbal tea, which he tracked down and analysed. He was pretty sure it must contain foxglove from the symptoms the patient suffered after she had taken it.

Withering was attached to Birmingham General Hospital, which had been established to care for the poor, as all hospitals were at the time. He was making a fine living from his general practice, an estimated thousand guineas a year, and could afford to treat (and experiment on) the poor for free. Over ten years he tried out different forms and doses of digitalis, very nearly killing a number of his patients, until he arrived at a formula, using not the root, but the dried leaves of a two-year-old plant. In 1785 he wrote up his findings as *An Account of the Foxglove and Some of Its Uses*. All Withering could do, however, was to give the results of his experiments, for he had no understanding of the chemistry of digitalis, and it was not until the twentieth century that drugs based on the poisonous plant were widely used. In the hands of Erasmus Darwin, who tried to claim it was he who had done the research on the plant, foxglove was downright lethal. His own medical notes testify to the fact that he administered fatal doses to some of his patients.

Withering had a stormy end to what had been a very successful medical career. He had become a close friend of the clergyman Joseph Priestley, a fellow Lunar Society member and experimental scientist. Although the Lunar Society itself had no political affiliation, Priestley and some others aroused anger by their support for the French Revolution of July 1789. In 1791 they had held a dinner in a Birmingham hotel to mark the anniversary of the storming of the Bastille in Paris. An angry crowd smashed the windows and went on to burn down Priestley's church, the New Meeting House, and wreck his home, setting fire to his library and laboratory. Withering feared for his own home, so got his servants to hide all his valuables. He also hired a private army of prizefighters and others to beat off an attack by an angry crowd. Four of the rioters were sentenced to death and two of them were hanged.

From the age of thirty-five, Withering had been sickly. He suffered from consumption, now better known as tuberculosis. After the riot his health began to decline noticeably, and convalescent trips to Portugal did him no good. He died in October 1799 with a lasting reputation as a medical pioneer, though his meticulous work on digitalis was little used in the century following his death. It was discovered much later that the action of the poison on the heart was what made it an effective cure for 'cardiac dropsy', but it was useless for treatment of other forms of the disease, such as 'renal dropsy', which was caused by a malfunction of the kidneys. Digitalis was also no cure for the disease that killed Withering, though it was prescribed as such for tuberculosis for a long time.

FRESH AIR AND GASES

There was a widespread belief in Withering's day that the best cure for many diseases in which the patient had a persistent cough or difficulty in breathing was 'a change of air'. That was why he went to Portugal. This was the first great age of the English seaside resort, and doctors would solemnly recommend Brighton or Scarborough or some Cornish cove as the very best place to go for a particular ailment. During his episodes of 'madness', George III was dispatched to Weymouth and rolled into the sea in a horse-drawn bathing machine (a Scarborough invention of the 1720s). He then had to drink a couple of pints of sea water, a recommendation of Dr Richard Russell, who believed the salts in it were beneficial.

Sea water was not a popular medicine, and the great majority of those who went to the seaside were content with the fresh air. Inevitably, those with a scientific turn of mind began to wonder what air really was, and what the difference might be between 'good air' and 'bad air'. In the eighteenth century what we would now call gases were still known as 'airs' of various kinds, or in the

Poor 'Mad' King George III was subject to just about every quack cure of the age for an affliction that was not understood at all: porphyria. He is pictured here at Cheltenham, where he took the waters. At other times he was trundled into the sea at Weymouth in a bathing machine and made to drink the salt water.

155

In his laboratory experiments into the effect of gases on animals, Joseph Priestley chanced upon what he called 'fixed air', which would kill frogs and snails. It was carbon dioxide, and he found the gas could be absorbed in water, giving it a pleasant zing and freshness. Priestley's 'soda water' was taken by Captain James Cook on his Endeavour *voyage.*

mines as 'choke-damp' (carbon dioxide) or 'fire-damp' (methane). One of the first attempts to collect different kinds of air was made in the 1720s by the aristocratic clergyman Stephen Hales, who wrote up his findings in a book called *Vegetable Staticks*. Hales found a way of collecting gases given off from distilled 'soups' of vegetables, as well as from hog's blood, beeswax, bones and gall-bladder stones. Bit by bit the component parts of air were identified. In 1750 Joseph Black identified what he called 'fixed air' (carbon dioxide), and Withering's friend Joseph Priestley, working in Leeds, found that this could be absorbed by water, giving it a pleasant zing. The result was soda water – the first artificially produced fizzy drink. Priestley's soda water became all the rage – James Cook even took a supply on the *Endeavour* – but he made no money from it. It was soon manufactured by a firm called J. J. Schweppe, and sold around the world.

Experiments with air became more and more elaborate as Priestley and others subjected a variety of animals – frogs and snails among them – to gases that often killed them instantly. It was discovered that plants behaved differently, and thrived in the carbon dioxide that killed snails. Scientists took to inhaling the various gases produced by burning minerals and vegetables, and went around sniffing the dank air of marshes. They followed their noses in the quest for a true understanding of the nature of the air around them, inspired not just by pure inquisitiveness, but the belief that they might find a cure for respiratory diseases, such as tuberculosis. For a time one persistent old theory got in the way: the belief that there was one combustible substance called 'phlogiston'. Scientists soon found that gases could be burnt, and nothing burnt quite so dramatically as Joseph Priestley's new-found 'dephlogisticated' air. This was re-named 'oxygen' by the French experimenter Antoine Lavoisier a few years later: Priestley had met him in Paris and told him about his discovery.

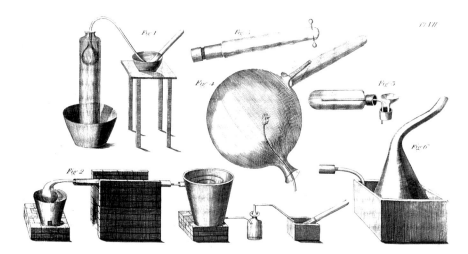

None of this experimentation did much good for the health of the scientists themselves, who choked and spluttered on their manufactured airs, but a belief that it might all lead to something therapeutic was reflected in the fashion for what became known as 'pneumatic medicine'. This was a special interest of Thomas Beddoes of Bristol, who, in 1798, opened a Pneumatic Institute in which James Watt, of steam-engine fame, was closely involved. There then occurred one of those extraordinary coincidences that brought together a group of brilliant scientists all intent on sorting out air, with some hilarious results.

The son of a Cornish wood-carver, Humphry Davy was born in Cornwall in 1778. His father died when he was a small boy, and his widowed mother kept the family going by working as a milliner and taking in lodgers. Davy had a patron who paid for him to attend a local grammar school, where he developed a keen interest in science, after which he was apprenticed to an apothecary-surgeon. Around this time James Watt (then working on engines for the Cornish mines) sent his son, Gregory, to lodge with Mrs Davy in the hope that the Cornish air would alleviate his consumption. Humphry and Gregory became friends, and when they learnt about Beddoes' Pneumatic Institute, decided to join him. The Pneumatic Institute was supported by most of the Lunar Society (sometimes dubbed the 'Lunatics'), and Josiah Wedgwood's son Ted was involved too.

At the age of nineteen Davy was in Bristol, having abandoned his career as a country doctor. He breathed in all the airs Beddoes could create, and discovered that one of these sent him into a kind of drugged trance in which he laughed uncontrollably. This was nitrous oxide, which quickly became known as 'laughing gas'. It was hoped that it would cure tuberculosis, but it proved useless as a medicine, as did all the other gases created in the Pneumatic Institute. Davy, however, noticed that it had a numbing effect and killed the pain of toothache. In its neat form, nitrous oxide was deadly, but if mixed with oxygen, it would produce only temporary unconsciousness. Experiments on animals proved this, so in 1800 Davy remarked, in an account of his researches, that it might 'probably be used with advantage during surgical operations'.

It is astonishing in retrospect that the discovery of an effective anaesthetic was not taken up by English surgeons. Instead, it became a kind of respectable drug craze in America, where groups of young people held laughing-gas parties, with the boys kissing the delirious and giggling girls. It became part of fairground quack medicine, with phoney professors amusing the crowds with exhibitions of 'Exhilarating or Laughing Gas'. A New York physician and dentist, William E. Clarke, spotted the similarity in effect between nitrous oxide and 'sweet oil of vitriol', a herbal that had been around since the sixteenth century. Used as an

Opposite: The eighteenth century was a time when many gases were isolated for the first time. Here is some of the apparatus used by the ingenious Joseph Priestley to isolate what he called 'dephlogisticated air', later called oxygen.

Nitrous oxide gas, discovered by Priestley, was initially tried as a cure for tuberculosis. The young Humphry Davy, however, noticed that, apart from making people laugh uncontrollably, it killed pain. But it was forty years before 'laughing gas' was used as an anaesthetic. Instead it became a fairground attraction, especially in the United States.

expectorant, the oil had become known as 'ether'. In 1842 Clarke administered it to a patient for a tooth extraction, which proved painless, and in the same year another American doctor used it as an anaesthetic in an operation on a cyst.

The demonstrations by Professor Gardner Colton, a fairground 'laughing gas' entertainer in Connecticut, attracted the attention of another dentist, Horace Wells, who offered himself as a guinea-pig for a tooth extraction. Colton administered the gas, and another dentist pulled out one of Wells's molars. He is said to have exclaimed: 'A new era of tooth-pulling', as he felt no pain. However, his enthusiasm for laughing gas was to lead to personal tragedy. Roy Porter, in his monumental history of medicine *The Greatest Benefit to Mankind* (1997), gives a succinct account of the sad decline and fall of this pioneer of anaesthesia. Wells had built a crude apparatus consisting of bellows and a tube with which he pumped nitrous oxide into the patient's mouth. 'Demonstrating it in the dentistry class of John C. Warren at the Massachusetts General Hospital, he botched the procedure…and his patient suffered agony. Wells lost medical support, grew depressed, became addicted to chloroform, and, after arrest in New York for hurling sulphuric acid at two prostitutes, committed suicide in jail.' Ether, rather than nitrous oxide, became the favoured anaesthetic in the nineteenth century.

VENTILATION

Meanwhile, the astonishingly inventive Stephen Hales, whose book *Vegetable Staticks* had inspired Priestley, set off in a very different direction in pursuit of the benefits of air. His interest in the mechanism by which liquids flowed through plants led him to speculate about the circulation of the blood, and he devised a gruesome experiment in which the amputated neck of a goose was inserted into the vein of a horse and the other end attached to a long glass tube. Changes in 'blood pressure' were measured by the rise and fall of blood in the glass.

Hales had a highly practical turn of mind, and invented many things. He was into pneumatics in a big way, devising a 'sea-gage', which could be used to judge the depth of water by the pressure it exerted. But none of his devices was quite so widely used and valued as his ventilators. To be healthy and free of disease, he reasoned, air had to circulate, just as fluids circulated in plants and blood in the body. In 1743 he published *A Description of Ventilators: whereby Great Quantities of Fresh Air may with Ease be conveyed into Mines, Gaols, Hospitals, Work-Houses and Ships, in Exchange for their Noxious Air.*

Hales first had the idea for providing confined and filthy places with a blast of oxygen-rich air when he learnt of an outbreak of sickness among soldiers about to set sail for America. They were suffering from what was known variously as 'ship, gaol or hospital fever', a kind of 'malaria', the general term for 'bad air'. It was, in fact, typhus, a disease carried by lice, but neither Hales nor anybody else knew that at the time. He missed that ship, but soon after devised a working ventilator, which consisted of a pump and a set of bellows powered by hand or windmills to expel stale air and draw in fresh air. It is believed that the very first ventilators were used in granaries for keeping wheat dry and thereby staving off various fungi that thrived in damp conditions.

Although the ventilator was tested aboard ship by the Admiralty and worked very well, they were not interested in adopting it. However, the owners of slave ships carrying Africans to America and the West Indies certainly were. Treated like so much livestock, slaves died in their thousands and were unceremoniously dumped at sea. Each diseased or dead slave represented a considerable loss of profit, and anything to improve their chances of surviving was considered worthwhile. The Board of Trade and Plantations therefore gave its stamp of approval to the Hales ventilator, and the American colonists were so much in favour that some refused entry to ships that did not have one installed.

Hales teamed up with a mill engineer, Thomas Yeoman, and began to install ventilators in gaols, where the death rate was notoriously high. London's Newgate Prison – the phrase 'as dark as Newgate's knocker' is still current among older

New gate

The windmill atop London's notorious Newgate Prison was installed in 1750 by the clergyman inventor Stephen Hales, who believed that stale air caused much disease, including 'jail fever'. The windmill powered bellows that worked a 'ventilator', which blew a breeze through the fetid cells. Hand-worked Hales ventilators were also used on ships and to keep grain dry in granaries.

Londoners – was the very worst. In 1747 the then Lord Mayor, Sir Richard Hoare, ordered a Hales ventilator for Newgate, but nothing was done until 1750, when a new Lord Mayor, judges, lawyers and six members of a jury were all struck down by 'gaol fever', spread by inmates from Newgate appearing before the court. By 1752 Newgate was being flushed with London air (none the cleanest at that time) thanks to an ingenious apparatus powered by a windmill on the roof that worked the piston and bellows below. A drop in the sickness and death rate of prisoners led to many other prisons placing orders for ventilators, and soon prisons at Westminster and Clerkenwell were being swept with gusts of Hales's air.

Hales did have rivals, such as the London brewer Samuel Sutton, who maintained that his own ventilators, powered by the draw of a fire, were more effective, even if they were more dangerous, especially aboard ship. The ship-board Hales ventilator, a box 10 feet long, 5 feet wide and 2 feet deep, was a simple mechanism that could be operated by manpower: a central lever, when pulled backwards and forwards, sucked air in one end and blew it out the other. Working at full tilt of sixty strokes a minute, it was able to move air at the rate of 3000 feet per minute, creating a refreshing breeze.

So successful were the Hales ventilators, which were installed in hospitals as well as gaols, that the Admiralty took another look at them, hummed and hawed for a while, and eventually, in 1756, ordered that they should be fitted in 'all Her Majesty's ships'. Thomas Yeoman, Hales's millwright, was appointed chief marine superintendent of HM Navy, and ten years later was still in post, fitting windmill ventilators to ships. There is no doubt that these ventilators provided the most successful advance in hygiene in the eighteenth century, though the theory behind them – that foetid, damp air somehow acted to 'choak up and clog the vesicles, and capillary arteries' – had no scientific justification. But Hales was no quack doctor, and the idea that fresh air was healthy had never been disputed.

160

SCURVY

The ventilation of ships at sea, however, appeared to have little or no impact on the most devastating of all ailments to afflict sailors in the eighteenth century: scurvy. The signs of this hideous disease – softening of the gums, blackened skin and a host of other symptoms – appeared to afflict the victims in no discernible order, and its similarity in some respects to venereal disease made it difficult to diagnose. Some believed it was a new infection picked up in the West Indies or some other remote part of the world. Others pointed out that it was referred to in ancient texts. What was not in doubt was that it had become a huge problem for the navy during the eighteenth century because expeditions were now making much longer voyages of exploration and discovery than ever before. Ships might be weeks or months on the open ocean, and it was then that 'sea-scurvy' was most likely to attack and kill the crew one by one. This even happened when British Navy ships had to guard the English Channel for extended periods.

Every quack in the business, as well as most eminent physicians and surgeons, offered the Admiralty a cure for scurvy, or at least their considered opinion that it was a result of sheer laziness, sexual excess or some other inadequacy of the dismal crews on naval ships. None of the cures worked, so scurvy remained something they had to put up with. That is until the astonishing four-year voyage of Admiral George Anson, which achieved triumph and infamy in equal proportions. Of six naval vessels that set out from England in September 1740, only one, the Centurion, returned four years later, carrying the single most valuable haul of high seas piracy ever recorded: thirty-two wagon-loads of Spanish treasure worth an estimated £800,000. That was the triumph. The tragedy was the loss of hundreds of men, most of them dying of scurvy.

The first cases were noted at the end of March 1741, and the sickness continued to spread. Anson wrote: '…as we did not get to land till the middle of June, the mortality went on increasing, and the disease extended itself so prodigiously, that, after the loss of above two hundred men, we could not at last muster more than six foremast-men in a watch capable of duty.' That was only six months into the four-year voyage. By the time the *Centurion* staggered into port with its treasure, about 380 of the original (and admittedly motley) crew of 500 had died of scurvy. Some of them had been Chelsea Pensioners and in pretty poor health anyway; others had been taken on as and when possible so that Anson could keep his ship afloat. Most of the six-ship squadron did not get home: of the original 2000 men, sailors and soldiers, 1400 died, only four being lost to enemy action. Nobody blamed Anson, who was soon to become First Lord of the Admiralty.

An illustration from James Lind's notebook showing a patient being bled – an eighteenth-century cure-all for everything from sore throats to scurvy.

Although most people were impressed by Anson's treasure, a twenty-four-year-old naval surgeon called James Lind was struck by the terrible toll that scurvy had inflicted on the enterprise. In particular, the detailed notes of a clergyman who chronicled the voyage excited Lind's interest. The Rev. Arnold Walters had noted:

> This disease, so frequently attending all long voyages, and so particularly destructive to us, is surely the most singular and unaccountable of any that affects the human body. For its symptoms are inconstant and innumerable, and its progress and effects extremely irregular; for scarcely any two persons have the same complaints; and where there hath been found some conformity in the symptoms, the order of their appearance has been totally different.

In other words, scurvy was a very peculiar disease, quite unlike smallpox or typhus, where the symptoms and progression of infection were easily recognisable and consistent. Lind made a note of this, and determined that some way or other he would find a cure, if not the cause. In 1747, when he was aboard HMS *Salisbury*, patrolling the English Channel under a sympathetic captain, Lind contrived what we would now call a 'controlled trial' to test the effectiveness or otherwise of a whole range of highly recommended cures for scurvy. He kept detailed notes and wrote up the results in a book published in 1753 as *A Treatise of the Scurvy*. Here is his own account of the experiment and its results:

> On the 20th May, 1747, I took twelve patients in the scurvy on board the *Salisbury* at sea. Their cases were as similar as I could have them. They all in general had putrid gums, the spots and lassitude, with weakness of their knees. They lay together in one place, being a proper apartment for the sick in the fore-hold; and had one diet in common to all, viz., water gruel sweetened with sugar in the morning; fresh mutton broth often times for dinner; at other times puddings, boiled biscuit with sugar etc.; and for supper barley, raisins, rice and currants, sago and wine, or the like.
>
> Two of these were ordered each a quart of cider a day. Two others took twenty five gutts [drops] of elixir vitriol three times a day upon an empty stomach, using a gargle strongly acidulated with it for their mouths. Two others took two spoonfuls of vinegar three times a day upon an empty stomach, having their gruels and their other food well acidulated with it, as also the gargle for the mouth. Two of the worst patients, with the tendons in the ham rigid (a symptom none the rest had) were put under a course of sea water. Of this they drank half a pint every day and sometimes more or less as it operated by way of gentle physic. Two others had each two oranges and one lemon given them every day. These they eat with greediness at different times upon an empty stomach. They continued but six days under this course, having consumed the quantity that could be spared.
>
> The two remaining patients took the bigness [outer shell] of a nutmeg three times a day, of an electra [paste] recommended by an hospital surgeon made of garlic, mustard seed, ad. raphan. [horseradish], balsam of Peru and gum myrrh [both tree saps], using for common drink barley water well acidulated with tamarinds, by a decoction of which, with the addition of cremor tartar, they were gently purged three or four times during the course.
>
> The consequence was that the most sudden and visible good effects were perceived from the use of the oranges and lemons; one of those who had taken them being at the end of six days fit for duty. The spots were

not indeed at that time quite off his body, nor his gums sound; but without any other medicine than a gargarism [gargle] or elixir of vitriol he became quite healthy before we came into Plymouth, which was on the 16th June. The other was the best recovered of any in his condition, and being now deemed pretty well was appointed nurse to the rest of the sick…

As I shall have occasion elsewhere to take notice of the effects of other medicines in this disease, I shall here only observe that the result of all my experiments was that oranges and lemons were the most effectual remedies for this distemper at sea. I am apt to think oranges preferable to lemons, though it was principally oranges which so speedily and surprisingly recovered Lord Anson's people at the Island of Tinian, of which that noble, brave and experienced commander was so sensible that before he left the island one man was ordered on shore from each mess to lay in a stock of them for their future security.

Lind left the navy the year after his experiment, returning to his home town of Edinburgh to finish his studies and go into private practice, but he dedicated his subsequently published treatise to Anson. Besides reporting the results of his own study on the *Salisbury*, he had much to say about scurvy, providing a rich collection of reports and anecdotes about causes and cures. He thought ventilation helpful, but favoured Sutton's fire-driven machine over Hales's hand-pump. The use of sauerkraut as a preventive was noted (a favourite of Captain James Cook), as was the value of fresh vegetables. And he gave his own recipe for making up a syrup or 'rob', as he called it, from stewed oranges and lemons. The acid in this might react with copper vessels and produce a poison, so he recommended keeping it in porcelain, the home-produced article having recently come on to the market in Britain.

With some disdain the Admiralty took a look at Lind's work, passed it on to the Commissioners of the Sick and Hurt, who then sought the advice of the College of Physicians – ironic, given that their own remedies had proved largely worthless. One member of the college was Dr James, creator of James's Powders, which sold over 1.6 million packets in twenty years and made him a fortune. He gave grudging support to Lind's claim about the efficacy of citrus fruits, while taking the opportunity to rail against the disgusting habit sailors had of chewing tobacco. Another Sick and Hurt Board commissioner, Dr Schomberg, was absolutely behind Lind's findings, but the surgeon at Woolwich Dockyard, a Mr Hill, dismissed citrus fruit out of hand. All that was needed to avoid scurvy, he claimed, was salt beef, a bit of vinegar and plenty of ventilation. In the end, nothing came of Lind's treatise until, out of the blue, he was offered the post of physician-in-charge at the Royal Naval Hospital at Haslar, Portsmouth. There is a strong suspicion, but no proof, that the man to whom he had dedicated his treatise, Admiral Anson, got him the job.

It was a long time before the navy finally accepted Lind's findings, though he gathered a great deal of support from other surgeons. Although Lind and others realised that disease was related to diet, and they had found a practical cure, they did not have any scientific understanding of the nature of diseases caused by a deficiency in the diet. In the case of scurvy, we now know that the missing ingredient was vitamin C. But it was not until 1922 that the polish émigré Casimir Funk, working in the United States, published his research on diet and disease, and coined the term 'vitamine'. Vitamin C was not identified until 1933.

Without any understanding of the vital ingredient in citrus fruit, Lind inadvertently destroyed most of the vitamin C in his syrup by boiling the fruit. It was also true, as Captain Cook was aware, that there were other ways of staving off scurvy. Cook favoured sauerkraut, and was anyway such an accomplished navigator that he rarely stayed in the open ocean without some fresh food for longer than was necessary. In his book *Limeys* (2002), which chronicles Lind's work on scurvy, David I. Harview argues that Cook's failure to support the citrus fruit theory held back the official adoption of lemons, and later limes. When the latter eventually came into use, they gave the British naval rating his international nickname of 'limey'.

The immense task of feeding the navy was in the hands of the Victualling Board, which reported to the Admiralty rather than the Navy Board. During the eighteenth century the standard rations of salted beef, pork, fish, beer and cheese were supplemented with oatmeal, sugar and sauerkraut (after 1782). There was also Mrs Dubois' Portable Soup, a concentrate invented in 1756. Just as doctors, whether recognised in the professions or out and out quacks, made huge profits from the sale of medicines, so those who dealt with the Victualling Board could make a fortune. With ongoing disagreements among navy surgeons about the best cure for scurvy, there was the commercial incentive to get your own brand approved.

Lind's study, which showed that citrus fruit, especially lemons and limes, was superior to all other cures for scurvy, was not accepted for a long time by the Victualling Board. This was partly because of the board's innate conservatism, but also because it promoted sauerkraut as an antiscorbutic, which was much cheaper to produce than lemon juice. However, more and more naval surgeons found that, whatever the cost, lemons and limes acted very rapidly to restore stricken crews, and it was the Sick and Hurt Board that finally put in orders to be paid for by the navy. Two Scotsmen convinced the Admiralty that this would solve its most pressing health problem. One was Gilbert Blane, who, like Lind, had studied medicine at Edinburgh and achieved high rank as a naval surgeon through patronage. The second, also Edinburgh-trained, was Dr Thomas Trotter, a naval surgeon with the Channel Fleet blockading France during the wars of the 1790s. Both were disciples of Lind, and Trotter was such a believer in citrus fruits that he once went and bought fifteen cases of lemons in a Portsmouth market when a Sick and Hurt Board delivery had not arrived in time.

Both Blane and Trotter became commissioners to the Sick and Hurt Board, and in 1794 began to campaign for the issue of lemons not only to those going on long voyages, but to the Channel Fleet, which was cut off from fresh supplies of food for long periods. From 1795 the navy began to buy citrus fruits on a regular basis, and scurvy became a rarity. James Lind had died the year before, at the age of seventy-seven. Some time later, Blane attributed the adoption of lemon juice in the navy to national prosperity, and paid tribute to the spirit in which Lind had worked:

> Are we to thank for it a guardian angel, presiding and watching over the dearest and most valuable interests of our country? Or is it more rationally imputable to some of those profound and exquisite discoveries in science, mathematical, chemical, mechanical or pharmaceutical, with which the present age abounds above all others? No such thing. The scurvy has been prevented, subdued, and totally rooted out, by the general use of lemon juice, supplied for the first time at the public expense in the year 1795, and which operated so speedily that in less than two years afterwards it became extinct, and has remained so.

BODY-SNATCHING

Naval surgeons were on-board doctors, who did more than treat those wounded in battle: they were general practitioners, and the same was true of country surgeons, such as Edward Jenner. The elite in the medical profession were the physicians who did not draw blood, and regarded the wielding of a lancet as 'manual work' and therefore beneath them. It was not until 1745 that the surgeons broke away from the barbers to form their own college. Although the range of surgery they could practise was limited in the absence of both anaesthetics and a means of controlling infection, the study of anatomy was regarded as an essential part of training. The top posts were in the charitable hospitals, where surgeons worked for

R.B.Schnebbelie 1830

no payment, but used their impoverished patients as guinea-pigs to establish a reputation that could be the basis of a lucrative private practice.

The education of surgeons required that they attend lectures in theatres, where the leading anatomists of the day would demonstrate their knowledge by cutting up a corpse. As dissection became an essential part of training, and each student was expected to have at least one cadaver, or the constituent parts, to practise on, the demand for dead bodies rose astronomically. Nearly all education was conducted in private anatomy schools in London, Edinburgh and other cities, where the anatomist could make a fortune in fees charged. To supply these anatomy schools with a sufficient number of corpses a gruesome trade arose in which all the leading surgeons of the day connived, paying grave robbers or 'resurrectionists' a good price for exhumed bodies.

The celebrated private anatomy school of William Hunter in Great Windmill Street, London, just off Piccadilly Circus, where young surgeons witnessed the dissection of corpses, many of them supplied by grave robbers.

167

Thomas Rowlandson's illustration of 1775 shows 'body-snatchers' cheating death and stealing a corpse from a graveyard. At that time, and until 1832, only the bodies of murderers were legally available to anatomists for dissection, but with the rise of new schools for surgeons, the demand for corpses greatly outstripped the supply. The gruesome but lucrative trade of the grave robber made up the shortfall.

Taboos about the mutilation of the dead greatly restricted the legal supply of corpses. Up to 1752, when a law was introduced to make the bodies of many hanged murderers available to surgeons, the official allowance was six bodies a year from the gallows. William Harvey, who published his findings on the circulation of the blood in 1628, dissected the bodies of his father and sister as part of his research. But it was not common practice among eighteenth-century surgeons to carry out post-mortems on their own relatives, or to leave their own bodies for scientific study. The resurrectionists supplemented the supply from the gallows, robbing graves in the dead of night and taking the bodies straight to the anatomy schools for cash. From time to time, the clinical detachment of the anatomist was shaken. In 1784 newspapers carried the story of John Sheldon, a professor of anatomy at the Royal Academy, who found to his horror that a grave-robber had delivered to him in a sack the body of his own sister.

This was a rare occurrence, for there were so many stories about grave-robbing in the newspapers that those who could afford it bought special locked 'mortsafe' coffins, put railings around the graves of deceased relatives and sometimes hired guards to protect a tomb until decomposition had made the corpse unsaleable. It was therefore the bodies of the poor, buried in shallow graves, that found their way on to the anatomists' operating tables. Grave robbers, if caught, were usually prosecuted for offending public mores because body snatching was not theft unless possessions were taken from a grave: the corpse itself was nobody's property.

The poet Thomas Hood, writing in the early nineteenth century, provided some comic relief with the last verses of *Mary's Ghost, a Pathetic Ballad*. The ghost describes to her bereaved lover what has happened to her body after burial, naming, among other well-known figures, the celebrated Sir Astley Cooper:

The arm that used to take your arm
Is took to Mr Vyse,
And both my legs are gone to walk
The Hospital at Guys.

I vowed that you should have my hand,
But fate gives us denial;
You'll find it there at Mr Bell's
In spirits in phial.

The cock it crows, I must be gone
My William we must part:
And I'll be yours in death although
Sir Astley has my heart.

The widespread business of grave-robbing continued into the first decades of the nineteenth century. Gruesome though it was, there is no doubt that the dissection of corpses by the leading anatomists of the day led to a much greater understanding of the workings of the body. The most distinguished anatomist of the eighteenth century was William Hunter, born in East Kilbride in Lanarkshire.

His father wanted him to enter the Scottish Church, and sent him to Glasgow University when he was fourteen years old to study theology. But at the age of nineteen, without getting a qualification, he left Glasgow to become the pupil of a surgeon, William Cullen in Hamilton.

Hunter, who never married, devoted his life to the study of anatomy, working in London hospitals, travelling to Holland and France, and establishing his own school and dissecting theatre in Great Windmill Street, close to Piccadilly Circus in London. An advertisement in the *London Evening Post* in January 1746 read: 'On Monday the 1st of February, at 5 in the afternoon, will begin a course of anatomical lectures. To which will be added, the operations of surgery with the application of bandages by William Hunter, surgeon. Gentlemen may have an opportunity of learning the art of dissecting, during the whole winter season, in the same manner as in Paris.'

Over the years, Hunter amassed a huge collection of preserved body parts, as well as medical books, stuffed animals, coins and other objects, which he bequeathed to Glasgow University, along with £8000 for the building of a museum to house them. After his death in 1783, the collection remained at Great Windmill Street for the use of his nephew, Dr Matthew Baillie, before being transferred to the Hunterian Museum in Glasgow, which was first opened to the public in 1807, and where, incidentally, the heating system was designed by James Watt. In 1870 the whole collection was moved on horse-drawn wagons to Glasgow University, where it remains to this day, the pickled organs, supplied for the most part by resurrectionists, still in perfect condition.

Hunter was one of the first 'men-midwives' or *accoucheurs* of the eighteenth century, and had a high reputation as an obstetrician, derived from his detailed study of the uterus. However, knowledge of anatomy did not lead automatically to surgical skill, and descriptions of operations conducted for large audiences of students before the days of anaesthetics can be horrifying.

Opposite: A cartoon dating from 1828, when the founder and editor of the Lancet, *Thomas Wakley, published a scathing account of a bungled operation performed by the surgeon Bransby Cooper at Guy's Hospital in London. Cooper sued Wakley, but was awarded only nominal costs.*

Thomas Wakley, the surgeon who campaigned against nepotism in London hospitals and founded the *Lancet* medical journal in 1823, published an account of a botched operation, the horror of which almost beggars belief. It took place in the theatre of Guy's Hospital in 1828, and was performed before a large audience by Mr Bransby Cooper, who had acquired his post of surgeon through the influence of his eminent uncle, Sir Astley Cooper. Wakley was not there, but was so incensed by the report he received that he risked a libel action by running it in all its gory detail under the headline 'The Operation of Lithotomy by Mr Bransby Cooper which lasted nearly one hour!' This was a procedure to cut out a bladder stone, which should have taken a few minutes.

One of the victims of the Edinburgh murderers William Burke and William Hare, who supplied anatomist Dr Robert Knox with bodies for dissection. James Wilkinson, known as 'Daft Jamie', was suffocated in Hare's boarding-house. Hare gave evidence and was freed: Burke was hanged and his body dissected.

The Edinburgh surgeon Dr Robert Knox who bought the bodies of Burke and Hare's murder victims. He was not called to give evidence at Burke's trial, but he was driven out of Edinburgh by an angry crowd who burned down his house. He died in obscurity.

The patient was Stephen Pollard, a fifty-three-year-old labourer from Lewes in Sussex, who was married with six children. Charity took him to Guy's Hospital, where he must have expected the very best attention. Instead he suffered a terrible torture. To prevent any struggle and to place him in the most favourable position for an incision to be made, Pollard had his hands tied to the soles of his feet, and his knees tied to his shoulders. As Cooper probed with his instruments and his hands in search of the stone, Pollard continually cried out for him to stop. The patient was treated, some remarked, as if he were already a corpse, for Cooper took no notice, grumbled that he could not find the stone, and when, after nearly an hour of rummaging, he produced the elusive deposit from Pollard's bladder, he took no notice of the man's cries. 'Never shall we forget the triumphant manner in which he raised his arm and flourished the forceps over his head, with the stone in their grasp. The operator turned to the students and said, "I really can't conceive the cause of the difficulty," the patient being upon the table, bound, while the operator was explaining.' Pollard died just a day later. After the account of the operation was published, Bransby Cooper sued Wakley, but was awarded a derisory £100 in damages.

In that same year, 1828, came the sensational case of Burke and Hare, the two men who made a living in Edinburgh not by grave-robbing but by selling the corpses of people they murdered in Hare's lodging house to the surgeon and anatomist Dr Robert Knox. William Burke, an Irishman who found lodgings with Mr and Mrs Hare, was not a grave robber, but he and William Hare knew bodies could be sold to surgeons. When an elderly lodger died owing money, they had the idea of keeping his body and filling the coffin with a sack of tanbark. Without much trouble, they recovered the man's debt by selling the corpse to Dr Knox for £7. 10s. Nobody asked where the body had come from.

This was easy money, and Burke and Hare began to lure the poor, lost and lame back to Mrs Hare's lodgings, get them drunk, kill them and deliver them to Dr Knox, usually 'still warm'. At least sixteen bodies were delivered to the anatomy school before Burke and Hare got careless, and the body of a woman they had murdered was found in the lodging house. Hare gave evidence in return for his freedom: William Burke was tried, hanged and publicly dissected. Dr Knox was not even questioned, but an angry mob burnt down his house and he fled to England, where he died in obscurity.

Before the Burke and Hare scandal, Parliament had been debating the issue of grave robbery with a view to bringing in some kind of regulation. The big problem was where to find a legal supply of corpses. From 1828, attempts to bring in a new law were thwarted. Then there were more scandals in which anatomists were sold the bodies not of murderers, but victims of murder. 'Burkers', as they became known, were at large in London. Finally, the Anatomy Act of 1832 made available to surgeons the bodies of parish paupers who had died in the workhouse. The unclaimed bodies of those who died in hospital were also available. A justification for this blatant prejudice against the poor was that, in the long run, the living would benefit from knowledge gained from the dead. But it was many years before anyone who could afford to be treated outside a hospital chose to go into one.

CHAPTER SIX

Cannon-fire

In the spring of 1804, an American left Paris, where he had failed to interest Napoleon and his commanders in new weaponry he had developed, took a coach to Calais and crossed in the sailing packet to Dover. As Britain and France were then at war, and everyone was acutely aware of Napoleon's plans to cross the Channel with an invasion force, the American at first gave a false name: Mr Francis. Once safely in London, he was able to enjoy the protection of influential politicians, such as the Earl of Stanhope, whom he knew well from an early stay in the country. The visitor's real name was Robert Fulton, and he had first come to England, from Pennsylvania, in his twenties to work as a painter. Among those who commissioned him were some of the leading lights of modern industrialism, including the young Duke of Bridgewater.

BOMBS AND TORPEDOES

Fulton had arrived in the age of 'canal mania' and, fancying himself as an inventor, took out patents for a sawmill to cut marble and a machine for excavating canals. Most of his schemes were of dubious originality and came to nothing. But he had been bitten by the bug of the machine age, and was determined to make his name with some invention or other. In Paris he had demonstrated his version of the submarine, which he called the *Nautilus*, and from which he hoped to profit with a scheme for planting mines that would blow up British ships off the French coast. The results were negligible, so he decided to try his luck across the Channel, or back in his native America.

From London Fulton wrote to Matthew Boulton at his Soho Works in Birmingham to order a steam engine, modified to his own specifications, which was to be delivered to New York. He wanted to devise a ship that would be driven by

A view of the entrance to Portsmouth harbour from the saluting platform in 1836. Two soldiers sit next to a cannon on an iron carriage, a pile of cannon balls placed nearby in readiness for battle. To the right can be seen the semaphore tower flying a flag signal. Beyond lies the town of Portsmouth, with its pier and Round Tower. To the left of the tower is the port flagship, the Britannia.

steam. As with all Fulton's ideas, he and his *Nautilus* were not the first in the field. In 1776 a young Yale graduate called David Bushnell had invented a hand-cranked mine-laying submarine called the *Turtle*, in a vain attempt to break the British blockade of New York harbour; and in 1802 William Symington had a steam barge, the *Charlotte Dundas*, working on the Clyde canal (see page 96). While staying in England, Fulton went to see both the Soho Works and Symington's barge, making notes about the boat's construction.

At the same time, he was trying to convince the British government that he had a potentially devastating weapon to see off the French fleet gathered in Boulogne, ready for the invasion of England. Through the Earl of Stanhope he got the ear of the prime minister, William Pitt, and was able to draw up a potentially lucrative agreement to develop his underwater bomb:

Articles of Agreement between the Right Honourable William Pitt, first Lord Commissioner of his Majesty's treasury and Chancellor of the Exchequer, and the Right Honourable Lord Viscount Melville, first Lord of the Admiralty, in behalf of his Majesty's government on the one part, and Robert Fulton, citizen of the United States of America and inventor of a plan of attacking fleets by submarine bombs, on the other part.

The government committed to an astonishing investment in Fulton's 'submarine bombs'. In a twelve-point agreement, he was to be paid £200 a month, with £7000 up front in credit, while enjoying the full use of any of the Royal Navy's dockyards and arsenals. An elaborate arrangement of referees would decide if his new super-weapon was truly effective; and if it were used successfully to destroy French ships, Fulton should be given a substantial part of the plunder. In return, he handed over all his drawings and plans to the Admiralty and promised not to divulge them to any other country. He had, in fact, two innovations to offer: the submarine and the torpedo, or floating mine. It was the second that appears to have concerned the government most, not so much because it felt the need for anything new in the naval armoury, but to prevent the French or other hostile nations getting hold of it.

A distinguished panel was appointed to pass judgement on Fulton's invention: Sir Joseph Banks, president of the Royal Society, the celebrated chemist Henry

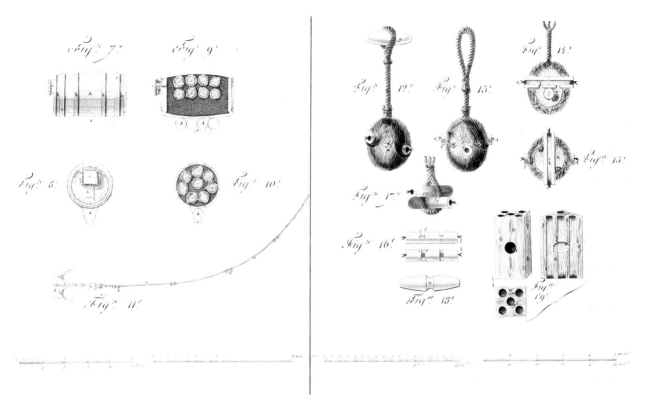

Cavendish, Major William Congreve, who had just devised a rocket shell, the engineer John Rennie, and, as referee, Captain Sir Home Popham. Exactly where Fulton's torpedoes were made is not clear, though it would have been in one or more of the naval dockyards that had skilled workmen who could turn their hands to making most things that floated.

Napoleon had built up his invasion force at Boulogne, and the British Navy had kept up a continuous patrol to prevent it from sailing. However, there were several attempts to attack it in the harbour, and the trapped invasion fleet was seen as the perfect target for the new torpedoes. On the night of 2 October 1804, the first employment of Fulton's new weapon began with a raid on Boulogne under darkness, with the flagship HMS *Monarch* leading the way. An account by an officer who took part in what was termed the 'catamaran expedition' suggests that the torpedoes, though ingenious in themselves, did not owe a great deal to the very latest technology in mechanics or construction. The 'coffers', as they were called, were made of thick planks, and lined with lead to weigh them down. They carried barrels of gunpowder topped with chipped flints. When they were filled, the last plank was nailed down and the whole contraption was covered with canvas and pitch. Inside was a clockwork timer attached to the flintlock of a musket.

Some of Fulton's floating mines that were captured by the French in unsuccessful attempts by the British to destroy Napoleon's invasion fleets in the Channel ports.

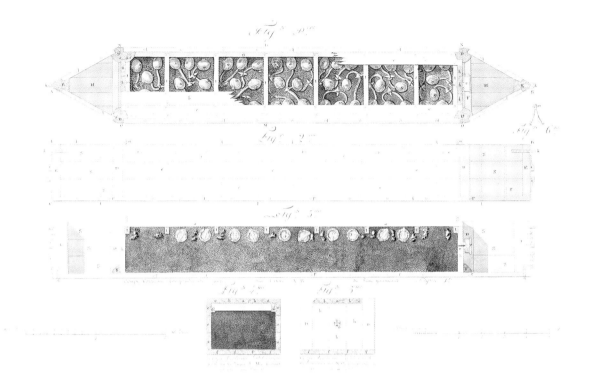

A French illustration of a 'torpedo' designed by the American Robert Fulton and used by the British in an attempt to blow up Napoleon's invasion flotilla in Boulogne harbour in October 1804.

The clockwork was set going by the removal of a pin, and a reward depended upon bringing this away. The coffers, some of which were 18 feet long and weighed 2 tons, were weighted with shot so as to float just awash and so escape observation. To each coffer were attached two lines, floated with pieces of cork, one a tow line and the other a grapnel. The latter was intended to be hooked on the cable by which a ship was riding at anchor, when the coffer would swing round by the tide and lay alongside. The coffer was taken in tow by a 'catamaran' consisting of two pieces of timber about 9 feet long and 9 inches square placed parallel to one another at such a distance as to receive a man to sit between them on a bar which admitted of his sinking nearly flush with the water and occasionally immersing himself so as to prevent his being seen in the dark or by moonlight.

The sailor guiding the deadly weapon was dressed in dark clothing, and it was his job to attach the torpedo to the ropes holding a ship at anchor and then paddle away furiously on his raft before the gunpowder blew up. That was the theory. In practice, the outcome was less reliable. When the raid on Boulogne was called off in the early hours of 3 October, only one small vessel had been destroyed, while the rest of the torpedoes drifted towards land and exploded harmlessly. Another attempt in December also had little impact. On 15 October 1805, Fulton gave his last demonstration, successfully blowing up a captured Dutch vessel (without crew) harboured half a mile off the beach below Walmer Castle near Deal. He had modified his torpedoes, housing them in copper shells. But the navy did not buy them and Fulton was paid off, not with the fortune he had hoped for, but fairly. Huffily, he wrote to a friend as he was about to return to America in the autumn of 1806: 'My situation now is, my hands are free to burn, sink, and destroy whom I please, and I shall now seriously set about giving liberty to the seas by publishing my system of attack.'

There were other new weapons tried on the Boulogne fleet. William Congreve, inspired by rockets used in India, had devised his own. It had a shell-like head and a shaft 6 feet long to give it some balance. It could carry a variety of warheads. But it no more put fear into the hearts of Napoleon's invasion force than the Fulton torpedo. Nor did hot-air balloon attacks. In fact, neither the army nor the navy was to put much faith in new-fangled weaponry. The major impact of industrialism on the technology of warfare did not come about until the second half of the nineteenth century, though some of the groundwork was laid during the period of the Napoleonic Wars, which came to an end in 1815.

One notable development, however, was the use of rifles in warfare. Whereas a musket had a smooth-bore barrel and could not be aimed with any precision, the grooved barrel of a rifle gave the shot 'spin', which made firing more accurate over a greater range. But muskets could be re-loaded more quickly, which could be an important consideration in battle. Rifles had been used traditionally as hunting weapons, and were considered too expensive and unreliable in warfare. Although they had been used in the American War of Independence, the smooth-bore, flintlock musket called a 'Brown Bess' remained the standard weapon in the Napoleonic Wars.

The value of the much greater range and accuracy of the rifle was, however, recognised, and in 1800 the Board of Ordnance asked for the principal gun-makers in Britain to come up with a model that was suitable for warfare. Competition was fierce, and the models tested at Woolwich came from the USA and the Continent, as well as from British gunsmiths. The rifle eventually chosen was made by Ezekiel Baker, a gunsmith in the Whitechapel Road, London, who already supplied the army and East India Company with muskets and pistols. It was pretty much like the other rifles on display, except for the 'twist' that Baker had given to the grooves in the barrel. But there were problems with it. His first models, which matched the musket in size, were too heavy, and he had to shorten them.

When the teething troubles were solved, the Baker rifles were issued to a specially trained Rifle Corps (95th regiment). These men were to act as 'skirmishers', harrying the enemy from hidden positions, unlike the regular infantry, which stood boldly in line or in squares, with bayonets ready, against an infantry or cavalry charge. For this reason, the Rifle Brigade was fitted out with green uniforms that afforded a degree of camouflage, with blackened brass buttons that did not sparkle in the sun, and the rifle itself had a ruddy-brown barrel and stock. The weapons were made, with slight variations, by a number of gunsmiths to the Baker design.

While there was a genuine interest in new weaponry in the early 1800s, the threat of invasion was considered a more pressing issue. Napoleon had assembled a force estimated at 130,000 on the French coast, and had more than 2000 small boats ready in a number of ports to bring them across the Channel. England's south coast defences were clearly inadequate, and there was anxious debate about how they should be strengthened. Fortifications would have to be built, but there was also the need for accurate mapping of the southern counties: and, by chance, this was already under way.

Part of the very first 1-inch-to-the mile Ordnance Survey map, published in 1801, showing Romney Marshes and the coastline between Folkestone in Kent and Rye in Sussex. It is known as the 'Mudge Map' because the survey work for it was carried out by Captain W. Mudge of the Royal Artillery.

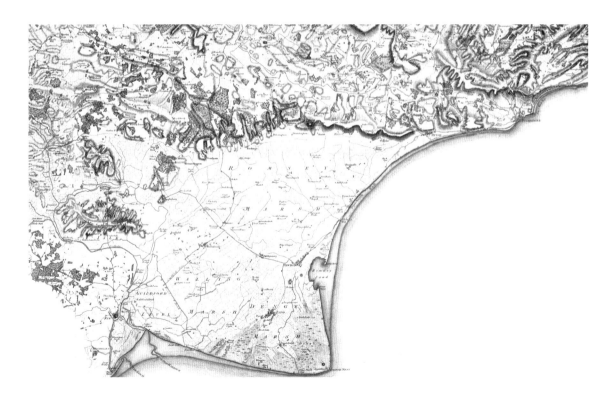

In 1783–4 the Royal Societies in London and Paris had agreed a joint project to fix accurately the difference in longitude of their astronomical observatories, and this involved basic map-making by the system of 'triangulation'. In England the task fell to General William Roy of the Royal Engineers. He established a baseline of 27,404 feet on Hounslow Heath, and by a calculation of angles was able to determine distance with great accuracy. General Roy died in 1790, but the Duke of Richmond, master-general of the ordnance, pursued the idea of mapping parts of England, and in 1791 ordered the very latest theodolite designed by instrument-maker Jesse Ramsden: it could read a mark at a distance of 70 miles with only a tiny error.

In 1795 the threat of invasion concentrated the minds of the military, and for the first time a full Ordnance Survey of the southern and eastern counties was begun. The first series of 1-inch-to-the-mile maps, based on surveys undertaken by the Board of Ordnance, covered the whole of Kent and was published in 1801 by William Faden, geographer to the king. The Board of Ordnance went on to survey Essex and publish 1-inch maps of that county in 1805. In time, Ordnance Survey maps would cover the whole country in increasing detail, marking every stream, windmill, church and post office. In 1870 the War Office handed the production of Ordnance Survey maps over to a civilian authority. Now, of course, they are a wonderful resource for ramblers and others who want detailed maps of any area of the country.

While the first Ordnance Survey maps were being printed, new defensive structures were appearing on the ground. A defensive canal was cut, which stretched the 30 miles from Shorncliffe in Kent to the river Rother at Rye in Sussex. The work was supervised by the master engineer Sir John Rennie. A military road ran along the canal, with gun turrets every quarter of a mile, and it was all finished by 1806 at a cost of £200,000. When William Cobbett came across it around 1823, he wondered at the folly of a canal built to keep out armies that had quite easily crossed the Rhine and the Danube. (However, the Germans treated it with respect in 1940 when they laid their invasion plans, noting where it would need to be bridged by forces moving north.)

There would be fierce fighting as Napoleon's troops came ashore. Plans to evacuate the whole south coast region were seriously considered, but rejected in the end by both the army and navy, as the flight of civilians and their livestock would most likely interfere with troop movements. The building of a series of impregnable towers that could withstand a long siege was suggested in 1803, but the questions of how many there should be, where they should be placed, how they should be constructed, and by whom, delayed the project for two years.

MARTELLO TOWERS

In the end, the building of forts was regarded as the most significant defensive measure, and, as chance would have it, the name adopted for these was taken from a fortification on the northern coast of Napoleon's native Corsica. Guarding the Gulf of San Fiorenzo was a sturdy fort on Mortella Point, manned by French soldiers. In September 1793 the French were driven out of the fort by HMS *Lowestoft* after a two-hour bombardment, which was part of a blockade of the northern Corsican ports. The British put in a Corsican garrison, but they were soon evicted by another French force. To re-take the tower at Mortella Point, two more warships bombarded it from close range, but suffered sixty casualties, including six dead. So the army lined up its guns and continued the bombardment from the landward side. It took two days to subdue this one, small fort. This so impressed a great many influential people in both the army and the navy that drawings of the construction of the Mortella Tower were made.

There were, in fact, similar small defensive forts all over the Mediterranean, and along the Italian coast these were often called *torri di martello*. Martello is the Italian for 'hammer', and referred to the fact that the alarm was raised in these forts by sounding a bell rather than by lighting a fire. Somewhere along the line, the Italian *martello* and the Corsican Mortella became confused, and all bomb-proof towers built by the British became known after 1803 as Martello towers. The original tower at Mortella Point in Corsica was blown up by the British in 1796, its walls – 15 feet thick – reduced to rubble.

The first imitations of the Mortella Point tower were built not on the south coast of England, but on the Cape in South Africa, as a defence against the Dutch and the French. There were also fifteen built on the island of Minorca in 1798. As more were built, a design evolved, though the towers were never identical. After a great deal of argument, the first towers to form the defence of mainland Britain were begun on the south coast in the spring of 1805, each of them given a number rather than a name. In all, 103 went up to defend the south and east coasts. Tower number one was built atop a cliff 200 feet high at East Wear Bay near Folkestone.

The walls of these towers were immensely strong, usually 13 feet thick at the base, tapering to 6 feet at the top on the seaward side, and 5 feet on the side facing the land. At the top was the firing platform designed to carry a long-barrelled cannon, and shorter carronades. Below that were the living quarters, then the stores of food to withstand a siege, and on the ground level were the gunpowder and ammunition, with a pulley system through the centre to raise these to the firing platform. The only entrance was high above ground level, reached by a ladder that could be drawn in. None of the towers was perfectly round: they were

Opposite: J. M. W. Turner's 1811 painting of the coastline near Bexhill in Sussex shows some of the Martello towers that were built to defend Britain in the event of invasion by Napoleon. From these vantage points overlooking the Channel, garrisons of troops could bombard incoming ships.

elliptical, with the thickest and more pointed wall facing the sea. General William Twiss of the Royal Engineers, in charge of the Martello building programme, wanted them spaced so that the shots fired from them would intersect, thus covering all possible landing areas.

After tests at Woolwich Arsenal, in which volleys of cannon balls were aimed at walls of different construction, the building material chosen was brick held together with an exceptionally strong mortar made from hot tallow, ash and lime. This so-called 'hot lime' binding set rock hard. There was certainly nothing the French could have thrown at these towers that would have made a dent in them. Many of the bricks came from London, shipped down the Thames and along the coast. And they were not cheap to build. Many have survived to be converted into homes, and the owner of one of these, an architect called Ronald Ward, estimated in 1968 that his tower (number thirteen at Hythe) had enough bricks in it to build thirty four-bedroomed houses.

Mortello towers were still being built when the threat of invasion was lifted, and had Napoleon crossed the Channel in 1805, they would have offered very little resistance. The towers remained impregnable anachronisms, and for a great many years they puzzled holidaymakers on the south and east coasts, as memories of the invasion threat faded, though there is now great interest in them and there are innumerable plaques on surviving towers, explaining their original purpose and history. Some towers have been blown up by local authorities that could find no purpose for them, but many remain as a reminder of how close England came to being over-run by Napoleon's army.

Napoleon's invasion plans were thwarted, as it turned out, not by any new weaponry or defensive forts, but by a superbly well-equipped and trained navy built by what was, in the early 1800s, far and away the wealthiest and most productive nation in the world. Britain's was a global economy, reliant on a huge merchant navy, which was protected by the guns of the Royal Navy. The loss of the American colonies hardly affected the spectacular rise in overseas trade at all. Its value to England and Wales in 1785 has been put at over £15 million for exports, and just under £15 million for imports. By 1800 this had risen to over £40 million for exports and £28 million for imports. The big markets for the goods of the new manufactories, such as Arkwright's cottons, Boulton's buttons or Wedgwood's creamware, were the United States, the East Indies, the West Indies and Germany. But they were sold everywhere there was a buyer.

To maintain this trade, Britain had to keep control of the Channel. This meant maintaining a permanent fleet of warships at sea, watching Brest and all the other French Atlantic ports. At the same time, to seal off French and Spanish shipping, there was a fleet in the Mediterranean alert to any movements of shipping out of Toulon or Cadiz. By 1804, Napoleon had his invasion plans ready, but there appeared to be no way he could get his army across the Channel. While Fulton's torpedoes and Congreve's rockets were being tested on Boulogne, the decisive action at sea had already begun. Napoleon decided to try to draw the British fleet away from the Channel by sending his squadrons based at Rochefort and Toulon to the West Indies. Vice Admiral Lord Nelson, who was watching Toulon, saw the French fleet sail on 30 March 1805, and followed, chasing them all the way to Trinidad and Tobago and back again.

When in the West Indies, Nelson noted that the French, commanded by Admiral Pierre Villeneuve, were headed back to the English Channel, and realised that he had been drawn away as part of Napoleon's plans for invasion. Unable to overtake Villeneuve himself, he sent a fast ship ahead, which alerted the Admiralty to the threat and predicted that the French would head for northern Spain. By the time Villeneuve rejoined the invasion flotilla, the British were ready for him and Napoleon's plans were abandoned. Villeneuve retreated from northern Spain to the base of Cadiz on the southern coast, where he re-grouped and joined a Spanish force. Nelson followed, and by September 1805, he and Lord Collingwood, who had been in command of the Channel Fleet, were blockading Cadiz.

The French and their Spanish allies were now trapped. On 20 October Admiral Villeneuve took the decision to break out and head for the Mediterranean. His combined fleet comprised thirty-three warships. Nelson and Collingwood had only twenty-seven ships, but they took on the French with confidence. They knew they were superior in training, tactics and fire-power. Once he had sighted the French at sea, Nelson called all his captains to dinner on his ship, the *Victory*. He explained the tactics: the enemy fleet would be stretched out in a long, ragged line; the British would attack in two columns, running in among the French at right angles; he would lead one column in the *Victory*, Lord Collingwood a second in the *Royal Sovereign*; they would get among the French and fire at close quarters. If signalling became impossible because of smoke and confusion, Nelson advised, '…no captain can do very wrong if he places his ship alongside the enemy'.

On the following morning, 21 October, the British fleet set out to engage the Allied (French and Spanish) fleet. Signalling was by colour-coded flags, each one representing a number, which in turn represented a word. England was 253. Nelson had hoisted on the *Victory* the message 'England expects every man will do his duty'. When the signal was noted down on a slate and reported there were great cheers, though Lord Collingwood wondered if there was any point in it. Four minutes later, at noon, that message was blowing in the sea breeze when the

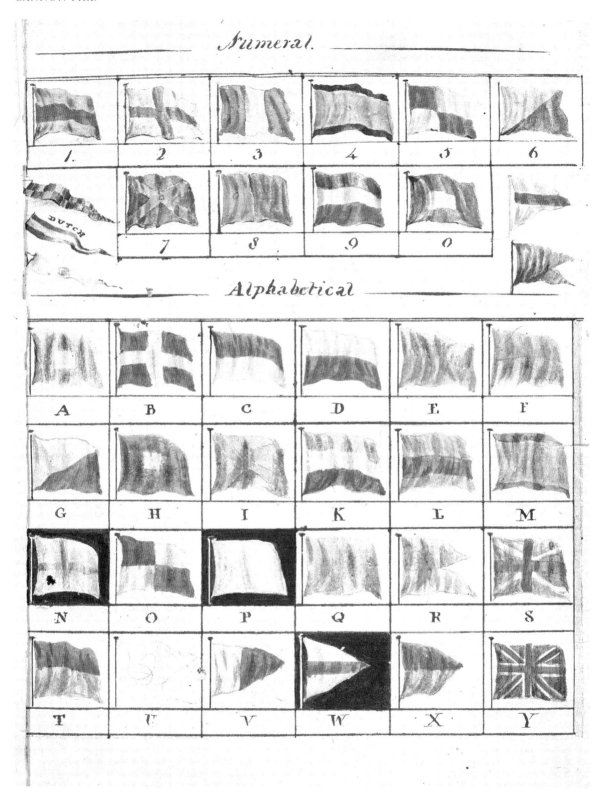

Victory and the *Royal Sovereign* ran into the Allied lines a few miles off Cape Trafalgar on the southern coast of Spain.

In sea battles at that time few ships were sunk, and the range of the gunfire was very limited. From a few hundred yards with a long-barrelled cannon it was possible to destroy a mast and inflict some damage. But most of the firing was at point-blank range, less than 200 yards, a distance that did not require the gun to be tilted upwards to reach its target. The *Victory* and the *Royal Sovereign* carried a hundred guns each, smaller ships of the line forty to sixty guns. The aim was to get alongside the enemy and pulverise its gun decks and their crews with volley after volley of cannon balls. Once among the Allied fleet, this is what the British did with devastating effect. It was calculated that the rate of fire of the British gun crews was double that of the enemy. During the fierce firing a marksman on the *Redoutable* hit Nelson with a musket ball, which pierced his lung and lodged in his spine. For three hours he lay dying and breathed his last just as Admiral Villeneuve lowered his flag in surrender. British losses were 250 killed and 1200 wounded. The *Redoutable*, whose sniper had killed Nelson, lost 578 killed and wounded, and the Allied casualties were believed to be over 5000.

Although Napoleon was not defeated, the threat of invasion was lifted, and the victory off Cape Trafalgar is regarded as the last great battle at sea in the days of sailing ships. The navy, which was rapidly re-built after 1805, was still absolutely vital to Britain's survival and its commerce, but it operated around the world, claiming key ports and territories for trade and supporting the land armies, which, in the next ten years, were finally to defeat Napoleon and leave Britain as the only major imperial power in the world.

Victory at Trafalgar was not just the result of brilliant seamanship, but was the culmination of decades of industrial growth in Britain, which outpaced all other European countries and enabled the governments of the day to invest in ship-building and the purchase of weaponry on a scale that would have been unimaginable before the middle of the eighteenth century (see page 190). Although of minor consequence in the long run, the fact that senior scientists, politicians and navy men were prepared to invest heavily in Robert Fulton's torpedoes was an indication of confidence in the nation's wealth. Not only were Fulton's experiments funded, but the agreement was that he would be paid £40,000 for his invention if it was shown to work, and £40,000 if he managed to blow up a ship. Offering this kind of money was not such a crazy idea as some of the older sea dogs imagined, for if an easily replicated weapon that could scupper a first-rate 'ship of the line' fell into the hands of an enemy, Britain's naval supremacy could be undermined. They made sure it was not much use before paying Fulton off.

Opposite: The Royal Navy used signal flags like these to communicate at sea. Famously, Admiral Nelson's flagship Victory *spelt out 'England expects every man will do his duty' as the fleet engaged the French and Spanish at the Battle of Trafalgar.*

Overleaf: The Battle of Trafalgar on 21 October 1805, as depicted by Richard Henry Gibbs. Nelson's strategy was to get broadside to the French and Spanish and destroy their ships at point-blank range with his superior fire power. For maximum impact, he led with the Victory *and two other ships that had three decks of cannon.*

IRON SUPREMACY

What was vital at Trafalgar, and in the many sea battles that had preceded the time Britain and France went to war following the guillotining of Louis XVI of France in January 1793, was the rapid growth of the domestic iron industry. The sheer quantity, as well as the quality, produced not only freed Britain from reliance on imports from Sweden and Russia: it made the country a major exporter and the biggest iron producer in the world. Although they were very particular about what they would buy, and put new models through severe testing, the Royal Ordnance could call on a vibrant and innovative industry to supply it with fire-power. One of the most successful new weapons was a short, stubby cannon called a 'carronade'. One of these – a massive 64-pounder loaded with 500 musket balls – was mounted on Nelson's *Victory* and fired the first shot at Trafalgar, wrecking the stern of Admiral Villeneuve's *Bucentaure*. The carronade was used by armed merchant ships, as well as by the navy, and sailors called it the 'smasher'.

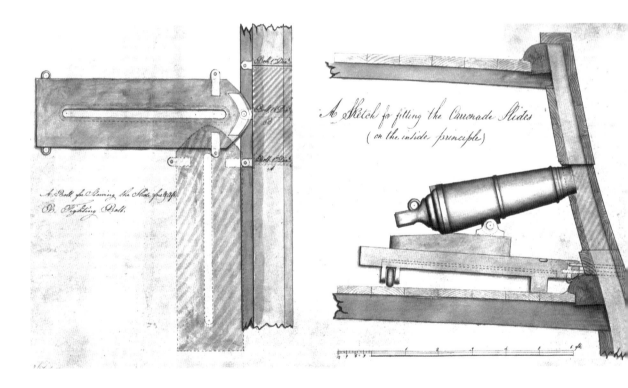

The carronade, known to seamen as the 'smasher', was one of the navy's most effective weapons. It was fired at close range and was designed to inflict maximum damage, its shot flying at a low velocity, which meant that it splintered timber rather than piercing it. Its short barrel and lightness made it relatively easy for gun crews to handle.

The story of how the carronade came to be made is a classic tale of Britain's industrial revolution. It took its name from the Carron Iron Works in Scotland, founded in 1759 as an entirely new enterprise that brought together the engineering and business talents of many people, and made use of all the innovations of the day. War played a part in its creation, inspiring a Scottish manufacturer to make home-produced iron, and fuelling a demand for more effective cannon from privateers and merchant shippers, as well as the navy.

One of the founders of the Carron Iron Works was John Roebuck, son of a Sheffield master cutler, who studied medicine in Edinburgh and at Leyden in Holland before returning to practise in Birmingham in 1743, when he was twenty-five years old. Roebuck had no stomach for medicine, and took instead to chemistry, through which he met a merchant called Samuel Garbett, who had an interest in refining gold and silver. They went into business together and began to manufacture sulphuric acid, then known as oil of vitriol, which was used in cleaning metals. Their Vitriol Factory in Birmingham was a success, but attracted the attention of Dr Joshua Ward, who had a patent on its manufacture. Roebuck and Garbett were storing their vitriol in large lead containers and producing it in much larger quantities than Ward, whose acid was kept in glass retorts.

Roebuck, knowing that Ward's patent did not apply in Scotland, moved the Vitriol Factory to Edinburgh, his student stamping ground. To make sulphuric acid he and Garbett imported sulphur from Leghorn in Italy, and saltpetre from India (supplied by the East India Company). Theirs was to become the largest vitriol factory in Britain. Meanwhile, near the works at Prestonpans outside Edinburgh, Roebuck and Garbett got to know William Cadell, a merchant and ship owner who had a business making creamware pottery. For this he had to find supplies of iron, most of it imported from Sweden. To cut costs, Cadell tried to make his own iron, as there was very little produced in Scotland. Roebuck and Garbett were also interested, so the three joined forces with the idea of setting up a foundry. They knew that Abraham Darby of Coalbrookdale had smelted iron using coke rather than charcoal, and set about discovering how these foundries worked.

As William Cadell owned large amounts of land in the valley of the river Forth, the partnership (which then included three of Roebuck's brothers) went prospecting for iron ore in the area in 1758. They found that there was plenty of it, as well as ample deposits of coal. For power they looked to the tributaries of the Forth, and Cadell found the ideal spot on the Carron river near Falkirk. Within two years the partners had put the works together with imported mill-wheels, skilled labour poached from Coalbrookdale and a steam engine, and bought rights to extract iron ore and coal from the local lairds. They also leased woodland for charcoal-making, as this was still used in the 'fining' process needed for turning pig-iron into wrought iron. When all was ready, Cadell's son became works manager, and John Roebuck went off to England looking for orders. He was writing back as early as 1760 to enquire how many cannon balls could be made at one firing.

The Carron foundry was happy to make anything anyone would buy. By 1762 they were producing all kinds of pots and pans for the home market, and exporting them too. A popular item was the 'sad iron', 'sad' being an old word for 'heavy', which was heated on the stove. The company made profits, had poor years, and many problems with the quality of their goods. They had begun making cannons for the navy early on, but these proved to be of poor quality, especially their 'long guns', which in testing at Woolwich Arsenal frequently blew up.

It was around this time that the old method of making cannon in moulds was replaced by ironmaster John Wilkinson's pioneering method of accurately boring into a solid brass or iron piece to create the barrel. It took some time to perfect this process, but in the end it produced a lighter gun that needed less gunpowder. The fit between ball and barrel was much better in bored cannon than in cast ones.

It was with this new technology that the Carron Iron Works, now managed by Garbett's son-in-law, Charles Gascoigne, developed the carronade. Exactly who came up with the idea for the 'smasher' is disputed, but by 1778 the new weapon was being tested. Two years earlier, the Board of Ordnance, which approved the navy's guns, had decreed that it would accept only cannon 'bored out of solid'. The carronades sold well to merchant ships, to the Russian Navy, and to the British Navy, which first used them to devastating effect in a sea battle in 1782 against the French. By that time the Carron Works were huge, one of the wonders of the industrial age, with many blast furnaces, steam engines, mill-wheels and dams, the building of which had involved many of the inventive brains of the age. An attempt had been made to bore a cylinder for James Watt's first modified steam engines, but it was a failure. Roebuck knew James Watt well and was probably the first to introduce him to his future partner Matthew Boulton in Birmingham.

NEW IRON FROM OLD

At about the time the first carronades were being turned out, Henry Cort, a former agent for the navy in London, had set his mind to the problem of producing high-quality wrought iron in England with coal rather than charcoal as the fuel. Cast iron was fine for making columns that had to withstand compression, but not for beams, chains, screws and hoops, for which the tensile strength of wrought iron was needed. The Darbys and others used coke to smelt

Opposite: A variety of clamps and drill bits for boring cannon from solid blocks of metal. The technique of boring – first patented by John Wilkinson in 1776 – greatly improved the accuracy of cannon, which, in turn, made for more efficient use of gunpowder.

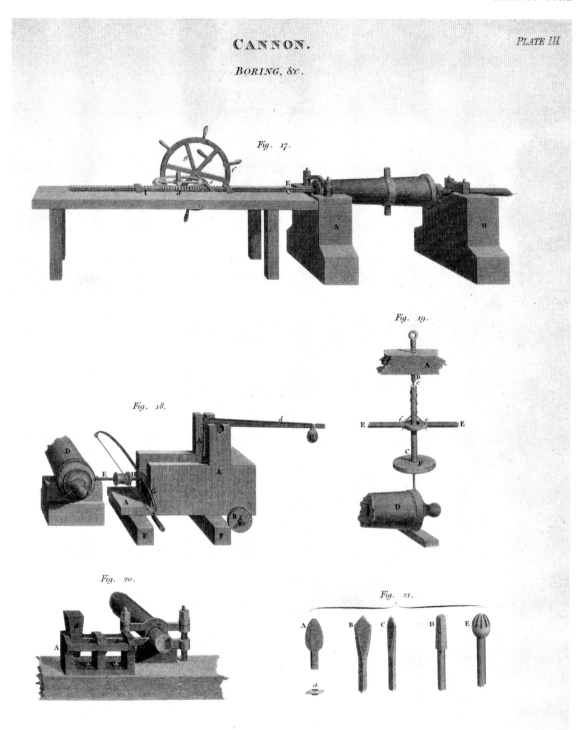

CANNON.

BORING, &c.

PLATE III

Fig. 17.

Fig. 18.

Fig. 19.

Fig. 20.

Fig. 21.

Jun.ᵗ delin.

Published as the Act directs, 1808, by Longman, Hurst, Rees & Orme, Paternoster Row.

Engraved by Wilson Lowry.

iron and to produce pig-iron in blast furnaces. But to refine pig-iron into malleable wrought iron using coal or coke, new techniques had to be devised. In the 1760s a process called 'potting', in which the pig-iron was re-heated in clay pots, broken into pieces and then hammered out, was invented in Shropshire, and widely adopted by ironmasters. But potting did not produce the quantity or quality of finished bar iron that industry and the navy needed, and much was still imported from Russia and Sweden. It was the problem of supplying Portsmouth Dockyard with iron barrel hoops that in time helped to transform the British iron industry.

Born in Lancaster in 1740, Henry Cort had made his way in the world as a navy agent, recovering prize money and back pay for officers and men. In 1768 he married the niece of William Attwick, who had inherited a thriving concern supplying the navy with iron goods: hammers, nails, shovels and the like. It was big business: in the year Cort married into the family they had fulfilled orders for 7000 items, weighing a total of 200 tons. Most of this was bought in: Attwick was not an ironmaster, more an ironmonger. In 1772 he left the business to a partner who, in search of new capital, was lent money by Cort, who was then still in London. In 1777 the Corts moved down to Gosport near Portsmouth, and Henry took over an ironworks at Fontley near Titchfield, with the idea of supplying the navy at a time when demand should be high: the American War of Independence had broken out the year before.

A big order came in for iron barrel hoops for the dockyard. Cort had to buy the iron to make the hoops, and much of it came from Sweden, which had raised prices to profit from British demand. He built a 'rolling' mill at Fontley to speed up production, and had to comply with an order to turn old barrel hoops into new. As this cost him a great deal of money, Cort asked for help from an old naval acquaintance, Adam Jellicoe, deputy paymaster of the Navy Pay Office, who was responsible for large sums of money. In 1781 they agreed a deal in which Jellicoe's son, Samuel, would become a partner in the business, and Cort would be loaned £20,000 at 5 per cent interest. Jellicoe would take half the profits.

To turn old hoops into new, Cort devised a new method of rolling old iron which was more efficient than hammering, and in 1783 patented the process. He then set about making his own wrought iron from scrap, and by trial and error came up with what became known as a 'puddling'. It was fired with ordinary coal in a specially designed furnace in which the molten iron could be stirred to rid it of impurities. The bar or wrought iron he made was much cheaper than that bought from Sweden. The Navy Board tested Cort's mooring chains, anchors and bolts over three years, found them just as good as those made from Swedish iron, and promptly ordered 150 tons' worth in 1788. As more orders rolled in, Cort demanded a lucrative royalty from any ironmaster using his patent methods, so it looked as if he would make a fortune.

Then disaster struck. On 30 August 1789 Adam Jellicoe died. It was discovered shortly afterwards that the money he had loaned to Cort had come from navy funds, and that he had given as surety Cort's two patents. There was £27,000 owing, and Cort was held responsible, although there was no evidence that he knew Jellicoe had loaned him embezzled money. By that time Cort had twelve children, and was bankrupted when the government demanded its money back. To add insult to injury, Adam's son Samuel was allowed to remain in charge of the business Cort had created. The only concession made to the inventor of a system of making high-quality iron was a pension of £200 a year. Cort died in 1800, miserable and ruined, and was buried in Hampstead churchyard.

Although Cort had not perfected his new furnace, ironmasters around the country had begun to experiment with it, in breach of the patents. James Watt knew of the piracy and, as a vigorous defender of his own patents against piracy, offered his support. He wrote to an associate in 1784:

> Though I cannot perfectly agree with you as to its goodness, yet there is much ingenuity in the idea of forming the bars in that manner, which is the only part of his process which has any pretensions to novelty… Mr. Cort has, as you observe, been most illiberally treated by the trade: they are ignorant brutes; but he exposed himself to it by showing them the process before it was perfect, and seeing his ignorance of the common operations of making iron, laughed at and despised him; yet they will contrive by some dirty evasion to use his process, or such parts as they like, without acknowledging him in it. I shall be glad to be able to be of any use to him.

Cort had travelled the country, calling at the Carron Iron Works among other places, to promote his novel puddling furnace in the hope that it would earn him royalties. But after Jellicoe's death he lost his patent rights, and the government that confiscated them did nothing to collect the potential income from them, which some estimated at £100,000 a year. The British ironmasters were free to adopt puddling without the cost of royalties, and after 1790 the new manufacture was adopted everywhere. British bar iron production rose from 32,000 tons in 1788 to 100,000 tons in 1805, and 150,000 tons in 1815. An order from the navy for barrel hoops had, by chance, helped to turn Britain into the leading producer of iron in Europe.

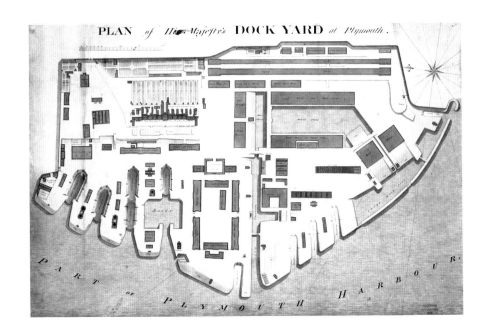

IMPROVING THE DOCKYARDS

The Royal Navy bought in a great deal of the supplies it needed, from carronades to anchors and iron hoops, and throughout the eighteenth and early nineteenth centuries was a major customer for many industries. Its largest dockyards, at Chatham, Portsmouth and Plymouth, were effectively naval bases, where the fleet would harbour in winter and ships were repaired in specially built dry docks. Daniel Defoe, visiting Chatham in the 1720s, described the myriad warehouses, gun-yards, rope-walks and timber yards as 'like a well ordered city'. By that time Chatham had been eclipsed by Portsmouth and Plymouth, which had larger harbours and were better sited for the Atlantic trade. In the second half of the eighteenth century all these royal dockyards were re-built on a grand scale, and employed many of the leading architects and engineers of the day, such as John Smeaton, celebrated for his re-building of the Eddystone lighthouse (1756–9). For the foundations of the lighthouse, Smeaton had made a cement that would set under water, a material that would prove invaluable in the re-building of wet docks (this hydraulic cement set by chemical reaction rather than drying, and was not entirely new: the Romans knew how to make it).

A major expansion and re-building of Portsmouth Dockyard was under way when war with France was declared in 1793. The Royal Navy was reaching the zenith of its history under sail, and the demand for all the materials necessary for equipping fighting 'ships of the line' rose dramatically. Essential pieces of equipment for manoeuvring sailing ships were the pulley-blocks used for

A plan of the naval dockyard at Plymouth. Here the navy took on board food, equipment and ammunition, and ships were refitted. From the time of its establishment in the 1690s it was an important naval base, which was renamed Devonport in 1843.

196

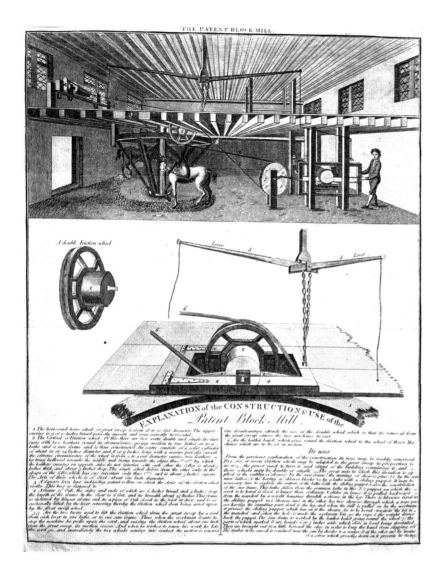

Old-fashioned, horse-powered machinery for making wooden pulley-blocks for the navy around 1794. Until that time, most of the work was done by hand. New machine tools developed by Marc Brunel and Henry Maudsley at Portsmouth Dockyard revolutionised the process and produced all the navy's needs with a tenth of the manpower.

tightening and slacking the rigging. The more pulleys there were, the greater the weight of sail that could be hoisted. A frigate in the 1790s might require over 900 pulleys. Yet each one was hand-crafted from a solid piece of wood, work that was very labour intensive. The navy bought most of these from contractors, just as it did metal hoops.

Although it had always insisted on the highest-quality materials for its fighting ships, the Admiralty became concerned in the last decade of the eighteenth century that it was falling behind in utilising the inventiveness of modern industry. It was prompted to abandon its conservatism by Samuel Bentham, younger brother of the philosopher Jeremy Bentham. Born in 1757, Samuel Bentham had begun work as a naval apprentice at Woolwich Dockyard. Noting his interest in the technical side of naval engineering, the Admiralty dispatched him on a fact-finding tour of the dockyards of northern Europe. He was then just twenty-three years old, but he so impressed Prince Potemkin that he was asked to reform the Russian dockyards, and even supervised the building of a flotilla of ships that won a sea battle against Turkey. He found the Russian dockyards very backward, so he began to devise machinery that could produce parts for ships without skilled labour.

When Bentham returned to England, he argued that the Navy Board should improve its ship-building techniques and update its dockyards. The Admiralty agreed, and presented George III with a proposal to create a new establishment 'consisting of persons skilled in the various branches of science… architect and engineer, mechanist, chemist', all to be under one inspector-general, who would oversee the better building, arming and victualling of ships. It was not easy to find a place for such a new post in the naval hierarchy, but it was created in 1795 against considerable opposition. And Samuel Bentham got the job. His attempted managerial clean-sweep in wartime was not well received, but Bentham's enthusiasm for innovation was to lead to one of the most brilliant and far-reaching inventions of the Industrial Revolution.

The navy alone needed about 100,000 wooden pulley-blocks a year in standard size: without them the fleets could not sail. Very few were made in the navy yards; most of the blocks came from two firms, Dunsterville's in Plymouth and Taylor's of Southampton. They did have some horse-powered machinery, but most of the intricate work was done by hand. Bentham began to draw up plans for mass-producing pulleys, though he was not skilled enough as an engineer to devise the machinery that could make them. It was while he was sketching his plans that a Frenchman, Marc Isambard Brunel, arrived in England in 1799 with his own blueprint for block-making machinery. Brunel was just thirty years old, but had already made a name for himself as an engineer and architect. He was born in northern France, the son of a wealthy farmer who had rejected his pleas to become an engineer and had sent him instead to a seminary. With the help of an uncle, Brunel managed to escape, and became a naval cadet, serving in the French Navy for six years until 1793. As a royalist, he could not stay in France after the Revolution, so he fled to the United States. In a very short space of time he began practising as an architect and engineer, working on canal surveys and establishing an arsenal and canon foundry. He eventually became the chief city engineer of New York.

Although he was prospering in America, Brunel had two good reasons to risk his future crossing the Atlantic to England. In Rouen he had met and fallen in love with an English girl called Sophie Kingdom, whom he wanted to find again. This coincided with his hearing from a fellow Frenchman about the problem the Royal

Navy had in meeting its needs for pulley-blocks. By the time Brunel arrived in Plymouth in March 1799, he had designed on paper a series of machines for mechanising block-making. He offered it first to Taylor's of Southampton, who supplied Portsmouth Dockyard, but they turned him down. Through a friendship he had made with Major-General Alexander Hamilton, who had been aide-de-camp and secretary to George Washington, the first president of the United States, Brunel was introduced to George John, the second Earl Spencer, who had been a navy minister and was later to be home secretary. So Brunel found his way to Portsmouth and the scientifically minded Samuel Bentham, who immediately recommended that the Admiralty take him on. He also found and married Sophie Kingdom, whose name was immortalised in that of his famous son, Isambard Kingdom Brunel, the great Victorian engineer.

Brunel had patented his plans for block-making machinery, but he needed the skills of Henry Maudsley, a lock- and instrument-maker, to design the machine tools that were made almost entirely of iron at a time when most machinery was supported in a wooden structure. It is said that Brunel showed Maudsley his drawings without saying what they were for, but the lock-maker guessed immediately. He made models of the machines at first, then got the contract to make them. Bentham had installed a steam engine at Portsmouth, which operated a saw and a pump, and he suggested to the Admiralty that its power could be used to run the block-making machines.

A pulley-block was a finely crafted piece of equipment. Inside the casing were two pulley-wheels, which revolved on an iron pin. They came in different standardised sizes appropriate to thicknesses of rope then available. The casing was made from solid elm, and the pulley-wheel or wheels from an American hardwood called *lignum vitae* (wood of life), which could be cut on a lathe to such a smoothness that it looked almost like a hard plastic. It was the same wood that John Harrison used for the workings of his self-lubricating clocks, and the bark was thought at one time to offer a cure for syphilis. To make both the casing and the pulley wheels, forty-five different machine tools were needed. They were set in motion by belts attached to revolving overhead shafts, which were turned by a steam engine. A new 30-horsepower Boulton & Watt model was bought for the purpose. By 1803 the first set of machinery for making medium-sized blocks was working, and by the following summer the Portsmouth 'factory' could make all the smaller blocks the navy needed. In March 1805 Bentham was able to report that they no longer needed Taylor's of Southampton, and their contract was ended. By 1807, with some slight modifications by Brunel, the new machines made every single block the navy needed. Ten unskilled men could do the work previously done by one hundred craftsmen. The output reached 130,000 blocks in 1808, and in 1810 Brunel was asked to calculate the saving to the navy of the new equipment. He said just over £21,000, and they paid him £17,000.

Brunel went on to open a sawmill in Battersea, with machines to cut staves for casks and to slice wood veneers. He also devised a way of mass-producing army boots with a workforce of just twenty-four disabled soldiers, and by 1812 his factory was turning out 400 pairs a day. Wellington's Guards wore them at Waterloo, and the Duke became a staunch supporter of Brunel. Over the next nine years, Brunel continued with an incredible range of inventions, from decorative tin-foil to a portable copying machine. But he was not an astute businessman, and in May 1821, when none of his factories was thriving, his bankers foreclosed, leaving him destitute. He was put in the King's Bench debtors' prison, and his wife insisted on going with him, leaving their children with a maid. Brunel was there for four months, until a rumour that he might go to Russia prompted the Duke of Wellington, among others, to get the government to bail him out with £5000 so that his genius stayed in Britain.

ROCKETING TO VICTORY

After Nelson's victory at Trafalgar in October 1805, Napoleon abandoned his invasion plans and marched on Austria and Russia, with disastrous consequences for himself and his armies. The British Navy commanded the Channel and tightened its blockade of France. It maintained the right to search foreign ships, including those now being built by the newly independent United States. Embargoes on foreign trade were ruining the US economy, but President Jefferson nevertheless remained neutral. But in 1811 a group of war hawks in Congress began to press for an attack on British shipping and interests in the Great Lakes and Canada, still disputed territory. Diplomatic negotiations were still going on when the president, James Madison, declared war on 12 June 1812, and ordered an invasion force into Canada, for which it was hopelessly ill equipped.

Britain's military resources were badly stretched, but that gave an opening for William Congreve to try out his new, improved rockets, which had not been much more than damp squibs when used on the French at Boulogne. The story of Congreve's fascination with rocketry brings together all those forces that fuelled the rapid progress of the Industrial Revolution at the close of the eighteenth century. His father, also William, had served as a general in the American Revolutionary wars, during which he had invented a new kind of lightweight gun that could be carried on horseback. He had fought all over Europe, and also discovered an economical way of making gunpowder.

In 1788 Congreve senior had founded a museum for the Royal Artillery close to the Royal Arsenal at Woolwich. This displayed the range of weaponry that had been collected from campaigns around the world, including war rockets captured in India. The maharajahs used them extensively for guerrilla warfare, often against the British, though they were in reality no match for European artillery. The powerful south Indian Muslim warrior chief Tippoo Sahib had an estimated 5000 rocketeers in his army, some on horseback, some infantry, the equipment being carried on bullock carts and camels. The British, who defeated them at Serringapatam in 1799, took possession of a huge arsenal – 9000 unfired rockets,

Not a firework display, but a 'rocketeer' preparing to bombard the enemy with a hissing incendiary. William Congreve believed that the rockets he made would be weapons of the future, but they rarely alarmed Britain's opponents in war.

along with 700 that had not been charged. These do not look much different from the larger rockets used in firework displays, the head being attached to a long bamboo shaft. One of the reasons so many could be made was that India had huge resources of saltpetre, essential for making gunpowder. The East India Company, which had its own standing army, imported a great deal of Indian saltpetre, and brought back some Indian rockets, which William Congreve put in his museum.

The younger William, born in 1772, was fascinated by these Indian rockets. His father, however, discouraged this interest and had him well educated. He took an MA in law from Cambridge when he was twenty-three, but never practised as a barrister. What he really wanted to do was improve on the Indian rockets, and this he began to do in 1804, taking advantage of his father's connections. General Desaguliers, firemaster of the Royal Laboratory, was known personally to Congreve senior, and had himself experimented unsuccessfully with rocket-making. Others who had also made rockets included the Irish revolutionary Robert Emmet, whose secret arsenal blew up, and a Scottish chemist called James Hume, who complained that Congreve junior stole the plans he had sent to his father.

The younger Congreve never claimed to have invented rockets: that would have been absurd, as they were thousands of years old. What he wanted to do was to make them effective in modern warfare. Firework displays were popular in late eighteenth-century London, and he began work with these. Then, using his father's influence, he was given the means to develop production at Woolwich Arsenal. Backing him were the Prince Regent, the future George IV, John Pitt, brother of the prime minister and master general of ordnance, and Viscount Castlereagh, the war minister.

On paper, Congreve's rockets looked promising. For one thing, unlike the navy guns, they had no recoil and could be fired from small boats. They were also cheap to make and lightweight. When he demonstrated them to Lord Castlereagh on Woolwich marshes around 1804, there was great excitement. They might be used to bombard ports around Europe: Cadiz, Genoa, Calais, Dunkirk…and Boulogne, where Napoleon's invasion force was awaiting its chance to cross the Channel. Congreve was given the go-ahead to make 3000 rockets, which he designated 6- and 8-pounders – the weight of the head. Twelve newly built 'rocket boats' were built, and these had launching ladders with hoops through which the wooden 'guide stick' slotted. Their range was supposed to be 2000 yards. Some rockets were incendiary, designed to set Boulogne on fire, and some carried shells that would decimate the invasion fleet.

That was the theory. In practice, when they were taken across the Channel on 18 November 1805, high winds made launching difficult, and it was apparent that they could not in any sense be 'aimed'. Some did not go off, others spiralled away harmlessly. Napoleon dismissed them as pathetic. Before his triumph and death at Trafalgar, Nelson had said he thought Congreve's rockets might annoy the French, but he preferred to rely on his trusted crews and the blockade to destroy the enemy. There was, understandably, a great deal of scepticism about Congreve's new weapon. But his patrons refused to abandon him, and he took them to the Mediterranean, where some were fired, and had a second go at Boulogne on the night of 8 October 1806. Congreve said he had set the town on fire, but the French dismissed the claim. *Le Moniteur* newspaper reported that two, which had fallen on buildings, were put out easily, and a large number had landed in the sea without causing any damage.

Still William Congreve persisted, in September 1807 taking rockets himself to Copenhagen, where the British were intent on preventing Napoleon getting hold of the Danish fleet. Again Congreve claimed success in setting the town on fire. This time others agreed that the sight of thousands of flaming rockets had been awe-inspiring, and the Danes themselves soon developed their own rocket establishment. In 1812 a British Royal Artillery Rocket Brigade was formed, and saw service in Napoleonic battles in Europe, notably at the Battle of Leipzig in 1813, where the commander, Captain Richard Bogue, was killed.

But it was in the war with the United States that the Congreve rocket achieved a kind of immortality. The Americans had attacked York Town in Canada (now Toronto) in April 1813 and wrecked it. In retaliation, the British sent a force to torch the US capital, Washington. This force included a Royal Marine Artillery Rocket Brigade with its specially designed launcher, the rocket ship *Erebus*, as well as a Royal Artillery rocket detachment. To reach Washington, the British force, mostly old campaigners from the Napoleonic battlefields, had to cross a bridge at Bladensburg. With President Madison watching at a distance, the rapidly recruited and poorly trained US soldiers set up their artillery to defend the bridge. They repulsed the first British attack, but when the rockets went off, hissing and flaring over their heads, they panicked and ran. That same night, 24 August 1814, the British burnt the White House. The British raiding party, with both ships and land forces, moved on to take Baltimore, which was defended by Fort McHenry. It was impossible to get in close from the river because the Americans had sunk twenty-two ships below the fort. On the morning of 3 September, a long-range bombardment began with fused shells, which were designed to explode in the fort, though many blew up in the air. Volleys of Congreve rockets rained on Fort McHenry too, but after twenty-five hours of bombardment there was no surrender.

On 24 August 1814 British forces torched Washington, the American capital, in retaliation for the burning of York Town (now Toronto) the previous year. A Royal Marine Rocket Brigade can be seen firing Congreve rockets from a specially designed boat.

Flying above the fort was a giant American flag. It had been made to order the year before by a Baltimore woman, Mary Young Pickersgill, who specialised in sewing 'colours', as military flags are known. With the help of her thirteen-year-old daughter, Mrs Pickersgill produced a flag that measured 30 x 40 feet, the background and pattern cut from 400 yards of wool bunting. The fifteen stars were 2 feet from point to point, and the eight red and seven white stripes were each 2 feet deep. Mrs Pickersgill's flag was easily visible from the British boats. On one of these was an American lawyer, Francis Scott Key, who had sailed under a flag of truce to plead for the release of a friend who was a prisoner on the British ship HMS *Tonnant*. Key got a sympathetic hearing: his friend was a Dr Beanes, who had helped treat wounded British soldiers. Key had with him a colonel who was an agent for prisoner exchange. But before Dr Beanes could be released, the British wanted to take Fort McHenry.

After a brief pause in the bombardment of the fort, the British began to fire cannon balls and rockets in darkness. Key watched and wondered if when daylight came the American flag would still be flying. And it was! Key fancied himself an amateur poet, and began to scribble a verse on the back of an envelope with the title 'Defence of Fort McHenry'. It was published in a Baltimore newspaper on 20 September 1814, and a month later, to the tune of 'Anacreon in Heaven' (a London tavern drinking song composed around 1790 by John Stafford Smith), it was sung on the Baltimore stage by an actor who called it 'The Star Spangled Banner'. The song contained the stirring, if rather clumsy line, 'And the rockets' red glare, the bombs bursting in the air, gave proof thro' the night that our flag was still there!' The Congreve rocket was immortalised when the United States adopted Key's verse as the national anthem on 3 March 1931.

Congreve himself was not in the USA to see what effect his rockets had. The Americans grew accustomed to them, and when they were used in the last battles of the war at New Orleans between December 1814 and January 1815, the American commander and later president General Andrew Jackson shouted to his troops, 'Don't mind these rockets, boys. They are mere toys to amuse children.' That was also the view of the Duke of Wellington, who wanted no rocketeers in the final, and close-run, confrontation with Napoleon. At Waterloo on 18 June 1815, Wellington instructed the small rocket brigade to carry guns. But a Congreve enthusiast, Captain Edward C. Whinyates, took some rockets along anyway. It is said that when the Duke was told it would 'break Whinyates' heart' not to be able to fire his rockets, the terse reply was: 'Damn his heart, sir. Let my order be obeyed.' But Whinyates was not to be thwarted. In the confusion of battle he managed to get his mounted rocketeers into the action. They set up their launchers in a field of rye that had not yet been trampled, and it stood so high that they could not see over it. Whinyates had the notion that he might support a cavalry charge by one of Wellington's troops, but he could not see where he was firing. Volleys of rockets whizzed up through the rye and landed somewhere, without any obvious effect.

Congreve rockets were still made after Waterloo, but apart from inspiring the American national anthem and frightening the natives in colonial wars, they were not regarded as a particularly effective weapon. When he was fifty-two, Sir William – as Congreve had become – married, but his health began to fail. He went to the south of France to recuperate, and died there in 1828 at the age of fifty-six. Many countries experimented with rockets, and they were used around the world until the early twentieth century. In Britain a new kind of rocket was patented in 1844 by the inventor William Hale. He devised a method of doing away with the rocket stick and producing a more accurate projectile by introducing a stabilising spin, as in a rifle bullet, at the launching. Hale's rockets were all metal and more effective than Congreve's but he had great difficulty selling them to the British Board of Ordnance. They were sold abroad at first, and were used extensively in the Crimean War in the mid-nineteenth century. But the early history of rocketry came to an end with the adoption of the much more accurate breach-loading rifle in the 1870s.

DEVELOPMENTS IN WARSHIPS

Robert Fulton's torpedoes and floating mines had less success than Congreve's rockets. Having failed to sell them to Napoleon and then the British, Fulton returned to the United States and tried to sell them there. Meanwhile, an alert British commodore who had witnessed the Boulogne experiments had come up with a scheme for protecting ships against Fulton's new weapon with floating booms and chains. So Fulton put his efforts into the steamboat project for which he had ordered a Boulton & Watt engine to be sent to New York. After a good deal of experimentation, his unnamed craft, which was popularly known at first as 'Fulton's Folly', made its first voyage with passengers, mostly friends, from New York to Albany on the Hudson river, a distance of 150 miles. The steamboat was later known as the *Clermont*. According to Fulton's own account of this historic journey on 17–18 August 1807, the outward voyage took thirty-two hours, and the return trip thirty. Fulton's steamer was propelled by paddle-wheels, and it was not long before he was ordering more engines from Boulton & Watt.

When the war with Britain broke out in 1812, Fulton had his commercial steamboats running on the Hudson and the Mississippi. He immediately came up

Although he failed to sell his submarines and floating mines to the British Navy, the American inventor Robert Fulton did produce the first passenger steamer, the Clermont, *in 1807.*

Opposite: While it did not see action in the war of 1812 between Britain and the United States, Robert Fulton's steam-powered battleship the Demologos *heralded a new era of war at sea.*

with plans for a warship to help protect New York harbour from the British Navy. It was an armoured version of his passenger boats, with the paddle-wheels set between two hulls to protect them from cannon-fire. But the war was over before it was completed, and Fulton himself died in 1815. What might have been the very first ironclad boat never saw action.

The major battles of the Industrial Revolution were fought, for the most part, with weaponry that had changed little in a century. At Trafalgar cannon balls and muskets shattered timber and sailcloth; at Waterloo the infantry 'squares' stood against the cavalry charge and flashing sabres. But these crucial European victories for Britain and her allies were only part of the story. By the eighteenth century, war was global, and after 1815 the huge increase in the wealth and productivity of Britain gave the nation half a century of clear world domination before rival powers began to match her industrial might. In war, as in peace, wealth was a powerful international weapon.

208

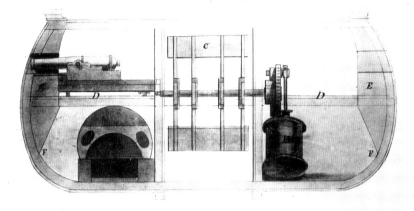

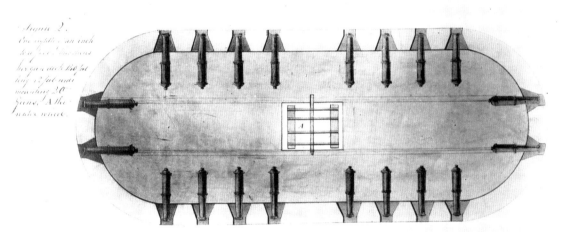

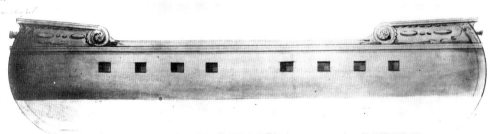

Further Reading

The great majority of works consulted in the research for this book are not currently in print and can be found only in libraries, second-hand book shops or through the Internet. It is possible to find some original material on specialist websites, and details of these appear below.

Of the books currently in print, Jenny Uglow's *The Lunar Men* (Faber, 2002) provides a colourful account of the lives and friendships of many of the leading lights of eighteenth-century science and industry. For an overview of the subject, one of the best studies is still Phyllis Deane's *The First Industrial Revolution* (Cambridge University Press, 1980), though it does not cover war or medicine. There is also a great deal of information about inventors in *The Collected Works of Samuel Smiles*, with a new introduction by Asa Briggs (Routledge, 1997).

Other suggestions for further reading are given below.

CHAPTER ONE: A POTENT BREW

The Arkwrights: Spinners of Fortune, R. S. Fitton (Manchester University Press, 1989)

The Birth of a Consumer Society, Neil McKendrick, John Brewer & J. H. Plumb (Hutchinson, 1982)

Cottage Economy, William Cobbett (Oxford University Press, 1979)

Fashion's Favourite: The Cotton Trade and the Consumer in Britain, 1660–1800, Beverly Lemire (Oxford University Press, 1992)

John Harrison and His Timekeepers, Rupert Gould (National Maritime Museum, 1987)

Josiah Wedgwood, Robin Reilly (Macmillan, 1992)

'The most extraordinary district in the world': Ironbridge and Coalbrookdale, Barrie Trinder (Phillimore & Co, 1988)

Power from Steam: A History of the Stationary Steam Engine, Richard L. Hills (Cambridge University Press, 1989)

The Rise of the British Coal Industry, John U. Nef (Frank Cass, 1966)

The Strutts and the Arkwrights 1758–1830, R. S. Fitton & A. P. Wadsworth (Manchester University Press, 1958)

For the John Harrison chronometer story log on to the National Maritime Museum website: http://www.nmm.ac.uk

Arnold Toynbee's *Lectures on the Industrial Revolution in England* (1884), are still

of great interest and can be found in full at:
http://www.socsci.mcmaster.ca/~econ/ugcm/3ll3/toynbee/indrev

CHAPTER TWO: NEW LIVES, NEW LANDSCAPES

The Arkwrights: Spinners of Fortune, R. S. Fitton (Manchester University Press, 1989)

The Practice of British Geology 1750–1850, Hugh Torrens (Ashgate Publishing, 2002)

The Strutts and the Arkwrights 1758–1830, R. S. Fitton & A. P. Wadsworth (Manchester University Press, 1958)

The Town Labourer, 1760–1832, J. L. & Barbara Hammond (Longman, 1917)

A useful website for further information about work and industry is:
http://www.cottontimes.co.uk/

CHAPTER THREE: STEAMING ALONG

British Canals: An Illustrated History, Charles Hadfield (Phoenix House, 1959)

The Green Bag Travellers, Anthony and Pip Burton (André Deutsch, 1978)

James Brindley, Engineer, 1716–1772, Cyril T. G. Boucher (Goose & Son, 1968)

Macadam: The McAdam Family and the Turnpike Roads 1798–1861, W. J. Reader (Heinemann, 1980)

Steam on Common Roads: Being a Reprint of 'The History and Development of Steam Locomotion on Common Roads', William Fletcher (David & Charles Reprints, 1972)

A good website about coach travel in the Regency period is:
http://homepages.ihug.co.nz/~awoodley/Regency.html

CHAPTER FOUR: THE LURE OF LONDON

Boswell's London Journal 1762–1763 (Heinemann, 1950, from Yale editions of the private papers of James Boswell)

A History of Regent Street, Hermione Hobouse (Macdonald & Jane's in association with Queen Anne Press, 1975)

Life in the Georgian City, Dan Cruickshank and Neil Burton (Viking, 1990)

London, the Art of Georgian Building, Dan Cruickshank and Peter Wyld (Architectural Press, 1975)

The Making of Modern London 1815–1914, Gavin Weightman and Steve Humphries (Sidgwick & Jackson, 1983)

Sophie in London, 1786; Being the Diary of Sophie V. la Roche. A translation of the portion referring to England of 'Tagebuch einer Reise durch Holland und England', translated and with an introductory essay by Clare Williams (Jonathan Cape, 1933)

The Third Man: The Life and Times of William Murdoch, 1754–1839, John Griffiths (André Deutsch, 1992)

Thomas Cubitt, Hermione Hobhouse (Macmillan, 1971)

CHAPTER FIVE: A REMEDY FOR QUACKS

The Conquest of Smallpox, Peter Razzell (Caliban Books, 1977)

Death, Dissection and the Doctors, Ruth Richardson (Routlege & Kegan Paul, 1987)

Doctor of Society: Thomas Beddoes and the Sick Trade in Late-Enlightenment England, Roy Porter (Routledge, 1992)

The Greatest Benefit to Mankind, Roy Porter (Harper Collins, 1997)

Limeys, David I. Harvie (Sutton, 2002)

Quacks, Roy Porter (Tempus, 2000)

A useful website about medicine and medical practice is: http://medhist.ac.uk/

CHAPTER SIX: CANNON-FIRE

The First Golden Age of Rocketry, Frank H. Winter (Smithsonian Institution Press, 1990)

Henry Cort, the Great Finer, R. A. Mott (Metals Society, 1983)

Marc Isambard Brunel, Paul Clements (Longman, 1970)

Martello Towers, Sheila Sutcliffe (David & Charles, 1972)

A Near-run Thing: The Day of Waterloo, David Howarth (Collins, 1968)

Ordnance Survey Maps: A Concise Guide for Historians, Richard Oliver (The Charles Close Society, 1994)

Robert Fulton, Engineer and Artist: His Life and Works, Henry Dickinson (John Lane, 1913)

The Royal Dockyards 1690–1850, Jonathan G. Coad (Scolar Press, 1989)

War at Sea in the Age of Sail, Andrew Lambert (Cassell, 2000)

Where Iron Runs Like Water! A New History of Carron Iron Works, Brian Watters (John Donald Publishers, 1998)

A good website about fortifications is: http://www.martello-towers.co.uk/

Acknowledgements

I would like to thank all those involved in the making of *What the Industrial Revolution Did for Us*. First, the presenter Dan Cruickshank, the directors Simon Baker, Jonathan Hassid and Billie Pink, and researchers Sarah Jobling, Nancy Strang and Edwin Blanchard. It was through the series producer, Patricia Wheatley, that I kept in touch with the crews as they filmed the programmes, and I would like to thank her for arranging books and some research material to be handed on to me.

I am also grateful to Professor Christopher Bissell, Dr James I. Bruce and Dr Alun C. Davies of the Open University for their very helpful comments on the draft text.

Thanks to Sally Potter at BBC Worldwide, who looked after the whole production of the book, and to Trish Burgess, who edited the text meticulously and in record time. Caroline Wood, also working at breakneck speed, found a wonderful collection of illustrations. I would like to thank her, and Kate Simpson, who helped me with library research. Thanks also to Charles Walker and Emily Hayward at Peters, Fraser & Dunlop for arranging my involvement in the project and looking after my interests, as always.

My friend Peter Razzell, an expert on the history of smallpox and Edward Jenner, provided valuable material for the chapter on medicine, and Professor Hugh Torrens was very generous with his time and research material on William 'Strata' Smith. As ever, the London Library was invaluable and all the staff wonderfully helpful. Thanks to them and to Simon Blundell, librarian at the Reform Club, who found some key books for me. Any errors are, naturally, entirely my responsibility.

Index

Picture Credits

If you are interested in *What the Industrial Revolution Did for Us* and you want to know more about the science and technology behind the Industrial Revolution, then why not study with The Open University?

LEARNING WITH THE OPEN UNIVERSITY

Since it began, over two million people have chosen to study with The Open University (OU), and for many reasons – some to develop their careers, others for personal enjoyment. The wide range of courses and qualifications allows you to create a flexible programme of study to meet your own needs.

Courses include:
* technology
* science
* humanities (such as the arts, history, geography, music)
* accounting
* business and management studies
* childhood and youth studies
* education
* environment
* health and social care
* information technology and computing
* international studies
* law
* management development and leadership
* mathematics
* modern languages
* social sciences

You can follow up your interest in the science and technology of the Industrial Revolution through a variety of Open University courses, including:

Engineering the Future (T173) examines what is 'engineering'. Introduces the context in which engineers operate, including product safety, patent law and current engineering practice.

Discovering Science (S103) serves as an introduction to science and covers a range of topics that broadens your understanding of many of the scientific concepts behind the inventions that came out of the Industrial Revolution.

*****Health and Disease** (U205) explores the social and biological factors shaping current and historical patterns of disease and health-care worldwide and in the UK, and includes a short case study on the impact of the Industrial Revolution.

*****Cities and Technology: From Babylon to Singapore** (AT308) provides a chronological and geographical spread over thousands of years, with particular attention to the impact of the Industrial Revolution in Britain, Europe and the USA.

These are higher-level courses, so we recommend that you first take a course at entry level to give you every chance of success in your studies.

Your choice

The OU offers a unique degree where you choose the subjects you want to study depending on your interests and goals. Alternatively we offer a number of specialist degrees. If you don't want to commit to a degree, there is a range of certificates and two-year diplomas to choose from.

Beginning to study

If you want to ease yourself into studying, our *Openings* programme of flexible, short introductory courses will give you the chance to test the water. Or you might be interested in our short courses, which last between eight and 20 weeks. These courses cover some fascinating subject areas, and three of them are linked to BBC television series: *The Life of Mammals*, *Blue Planet* and *Leonardo*.

Supporting you all the way

With the OU, you'll never study alone. At the start of each course, you are allocated a tutor and study group, who can be contacted by post, telephone or e-mail. Your tutor will provide advice and guidance throughout your studies, and will give individual feedback on your progress. Your Regional Centre is also on hand to answer any queries you may have.

Find out more

To learn more about our courses and qualifications, and to find out what it's like to be an OU student, visit our website at **www.open.ac.uk/firststep**

call our Course Information and Advice Centre on **01908 653231**
e-mail **general-enquiries@open.ac.uk**

Or you can write to:
The Open University
PO Box 625
Walton Hall
Milton Keynes MK7 6YG

For information about Open University broadcasts and associated learning, visit our website **www.Open2.NET**

The Open University has a wide range of supporting teaching materials for sale, including self-study workbooks, videos and software. For more information go to: **www.ouw.co.uk**